Sane Spirituality

Sane Spirituality

*Lessons from Corinth
for the Twenty-first Century*

Stuart Bell

Sovereign World

Sovereign World Ltd
PO Box 777
Tonbridge
Kent TN11 0ZS
England

ISBN 1 85240 409 4

Cover design by CCD, www.ccdgroup.co.uk
Typeset by CRB Associates, Reepham, Norfolk
Printed by Clays Ltd, St Ives plc

Contents

What Others Are Saying About
Sane Spirituality

'Don't miss this book. It's vital, celebrating as it does the wonder of charismata, yet lovingly inviting us "Charismatics" to some overdue housekeeping. Stuart shares wisdom, passion and down to earth common sense that will help us handle the stuff of heaven. It'll change your life and your church.'

Jeff Lucas
Author, speaker and broadcaster

'A book of excellence; thought-provoking, soul-searching, heart-warming. A "must" for any reader on a quest for church as it was really meant to be.'

Muriel Shelbourne
Preacher, teacher and author

'Stuart Bell's new book, *Sane Spirituality*, is an absolute must-read for anyone who loves the Church. Written with apostolic wisdom, this book demonstrates Stuart's love for the body of Christ and a longing to see us come to a true unity of faith. I believe we are all tired of talk and are longing for unity based on deep love for Jesus and transparent honesty. Stuart's prophetic insight will help anyone who wants to see the body of Christ without wrinkle or spot. Everyone in leadership needs this book!'

Melinda Fish
Author, teacher, editor *Spread the Fire* magazine

'With his clear love for the Word of God and considerable ministry experience, Stuart has produced a study of the

1st Century Church at Corinth that is both thoroughly read-able and highly instructive for the Church of the twenty-first century. It will undoubtedly help individuals and congrega-tions walk in greater Christ-like *character* and *charisma*. I heartily recommend it to you.'

Dr David Smith
Senior Pastor, Peterborough Community Church

'With warmth, straight-talking and fine balance, Stuart Bell writes as only a sensitive, experienced and insightful pastor can. He addresses issues of burning relevance for today's often jaded, disillusioned, and novelty-seeking churches. This is a brilliant introduction that helps us hear afresh the message of Paul's red-hot Corinthian correspondence, making it sound like it's just been written. The ink still seems wet on the papyrus!'

Greg Haslam
Minister, Westminster Chapel, London

Dedication

This book is dedicated to spiritual mothers and fathers in the Church and particularly to Gerald Coates: 'I will always be grateful for your love and support through the years.'

To Jean Darnall: 'For believing in me in the early days of my ministry and for speaking so directly into my life.'

Honour and thanks also to Geoffrey and Betty; Lionel and Betty.

Acknowledgements

Many thanks once more go to my family – Irene, Andrew, David, Becki and Glen. Val Seager for hours of typing and for being a faithful help to me for many years. Rita Blackler and Muriel Shelbourne for proof reading.

To my wider family for their support: Graham and Molly, David and Ann, David and Elizabeth.

Special thanks to Jeff and Kay Lucas, and Duane and Kris White for being such a support to us during the last difficult year.

To the worship leaders who have allowed me to use their songs.

Foreword

The publishing of this book finds an apt time and place. Currently so much importance is given to the notion that post-modern thinking and perceptions pose an ultimately unique and radical problem for the church. The truth is that much of what is described as post-modernity was alive and well in the prospering church of the first century. Corinth was home to a potpourri of vague pantheisms, spiritualities that permitted all manner of human behaviour and immorality in the name of religion. This was not Athens. Corinth was a consummate seaport. Science and logic did not hold sway here. People were thirsty for the supernatural, but not at the cost of any human constraint. The church in Corinth wrestled with a synthesis of cultures that were violent at times and factious. Cohabitation was hardly limited to faithful heterosexual marriages. There was no civil government with Christian values to be elected. There was no history or tradition that was sympathetic to Christians. It was as it is.

Stuart Bell's book is replete with references to the church in Britain. But it is pertinent that this foreword to his book is being written in America. The growing chasm between healthy biblical values and the abuse of spirituality and its consequences is a condition thoroughly shared with the North American church. The advent of the charismatic movement in the late nineteen sixties in America brought a Spirit-driven life to worship and practice that now extends to the entire evangelical church. Whereas early charismatic worship formats were considered profane thirty years ago, 'contemporary services' have become the order of the day for churches that that once insisted on traditional liturgies of various sorts.

13

The impact continues to be renewing and refreshing for the church. But inasmuch as congregations take on board the theology of the songs they sing, Corinthian experience breeds Corinthian problems. One is hard put to think of an evangelical pastor who would not benefit from this unfolding of the Corinthian dilemma and Paul's inspired response.

For the church entering the twenty-first century, Corinth has become our globe. The problems and tensions described herein are representative of problems and tensions in the global church. There are, to be sure, some ironies here. Practising Christians within the United Kingdom represent a comparatively small percentage of the country's population relative to nations such as Zambia, Guatemala or Korea. Nevertheless for historical as well as economic reasons, the charismatic church in the United Kingdom and in the West itself is theologically influential in disproportion to its Christian population. Compound this with the fact that the fastest growing sector of Christianity in the developing world is manifestly charismatic (or Pentecostal depending upon one's terminology). We discover that the tensions and dysfunctions addressed by Paul in his first-century letter are more globally relevant than ever before in the church's history.

There is another irony and it goes to the heart of the Corinthian problem and our problem. Cultures that are saturated in sexuality tend to find their families collapsed and their societies emptied of intimacy. Mother Theresa of Calcutta cited the loneliness of the West as a deeper human problem than the poverty of the East. In the following pages, the Corinthian problem is unpacked as Paul understood it – essentially a problem of the lack of love. The problem is love and relationship and family, the warp and the woof of the church itself. So an investigation of Paul's heart and thought cannot merely be a commentary born of some need to be analytical. The following pages are written by a pastor, like Paul, deeply encouraged by the truth of the power of healthy local churches. This is an apostolic book to a church with a need to have its heart realigned – to have the dots connected between healthy doctrine, healthy practice and healthy relationship. As it was with for brothers and sisters in Corinth, so we are in need of a heart that understands human dignity in terms of the sacrifice, humility and love of the cross of Jesus. Only with that heart are we ready to effect the power of His resurrection.

Jack Groblewski
Bethlehem
July 2004

Introduction

Some years ago I was 'cornered' by a well-meaning brother who, before introducing himself, looked me squarely in the eyes and boldly asked, 'What is your favourite scripture?' Taken by surprise and reeling slightly from his seemingly aggressive approach, I found myself unable to answer his question. I muttered a few words like, 'Well, I like all the Bible, really!' But inwardly I felt intimidated. He remained a few inches from my nose, but still no greater revelation came and the truth was my mind had gone blank. I had been a Christian leader for many years; as a boy I had diligently learnt scripture verses on a daily basis, but even John 3:16 didn't come to mind. The strange thing was I didn't even think to ask him, 'Why?', but muttered on, clearly leaving him with the impression that actually I had never even read the Bible! Through the years I have noticed that people want to put us under pressure to follow their agenda. I have learned gradually that I don't have to know as much as others, parade what I have learned, or be afraid to say, 'I don't know.' In this book I simply want to offer my perspectives with regard to things that have recently gripped my attention.

So, please permit me to stand to my full height (which I have to accept is not considerable!), take a deep breath and say that after serious thought, perhaps I could go some way towards answering the enquiry of the brother in question. 'Favourite' is not quite the right word, but may I offer two books from the Old Testament and two from the New. I choose these because I believe they speak directly into today's church scene. The books from the Old Testament are Ezra and Nehemiah; I have already written a book on the issues they raise called *Rebuilding the Walls* (Sovereign World, 2003). From the New Testament I have now chosen Paul's letters to the church at Corinth. When I was first thrust into church planting I continually looked into the Scriptures to see how the early church operated. Time and again I read through the Acts of the Apostles, and with an increasing number of questions concerning the gifts of the Spirit, the Body of Christ and New Testament worship I avidly read through 1 Corinthians. These verses became foundational to how we operated and Paul's teaching gave us a deep desire to see a thoroughly 'charismatic' church emerge. Almost three decades have since passed, but I believe Paul's letters are even more relevant to the church today than they were then.

Throughout this book I make reference to the 'British scene', because it is the part of the church I know best. However, I believe that the things I will share have wider implications for the church at large and particularly to the church in the West.

Chapter 1

Challenges Facing Charismatics

At the beginning of 2002, I embarked on a series of teachings at New Life Christian Fellowship in Lincoln under the title 'Corinth – a challenge to charismatics'. This was due to a number of things that caught my attention. I had a growing concern over certain characteristics that seemed to be impacting the British churches. I was also aware of an apparent acceleration in the decline of certain fellowships and movements. As these things dominated my thinking, I found myself studying Paul's letters to the church at Corinth. As I read through 1 Corinthians I felt its contents were very challenging. I believe that this teaching is relevant to all churches, but was keenly aware that I needed to apply God's word into the part of the church I know best, the charismatic sector. I will give definition to the term 'charismatic' as I move on and hope to paint a picture of what a truly charismatic church should look like, but I think it is always a healthy thing to begin with ourselves and what we represent. So, in setting the scene, I would like to highlight some of the reasons why I gave time to this series.

The gap

I was becoming increasingly aware of a growing gap between character and gift in the lives of individuals and churches. All of us have been saddened when highly gifted people have been found to be living a double life. When heroes fall many people are affected. It feels as though our trust has been betrayed, and trust is one of the hardest things to rebuild. The Bible says that when shepherds are removed their flocks are scattered. Sadly, it is possible for people to exhibit spiritual gifts, even move in spiritual power, and still be deceived. At a lower level, there is a gap between people's spiritual values and their behaviour. Some of the rudest people I have met are Christians and that ought not to be!

Fragmentation

I have also observed over recent years a tendency towards fragmentation in a number of churches. Churches that once stood strong with effective ministries into towns and cities have found their resources dissipated. Rightly we have been challenged by some to look at what church is really all about. It is a healthy thing to ask fundamental questions about the nature of church. However, in the process, initiatives that in themselves sound radical and creative, but actually have elements of division and partiality within them, have affected a number of churches. I have become nervous of phrases that sound harmless or even helpful, yet carry small destructive seeds if pushed to extremes. Such phrases as 'we are churching it at ... ' rightly emphasise that the church is 'people', but wrongly defines a group discussion at McDonalds or the local pub as 'church'. Church is more than having a chat over coffee. Even 'reinventing church' sounds good, but implies that everything to do with the present structure of church needs demolishing.

Unfortunately, such polarised positions are not helping church unity and 'invisible' churches are not easily led or overseen. The advocates of this position of course look with suspicion at oversight and would be nervous of strong leadership. Even putting these thoughts in print lines me up with the 'old guard' who don't really understand the arguments. However, I am sure that the gathered church is still on God's agenda and it is interesting to me that this is a vital element in countries that are experiencing revival at this time. Though I am strong on these things, I do want to remain open to learn and to listen to the viewpoint of others. I certainly don't wish to add to the polarisation

Disillusionment

I have also observed in certain quarters of the church a measure of disillusionment in the aftermath of various moves of the Spirit. Toronto and Pensacola were both places of refreshing and the moving of the Holy Spirit from 1994 onward. Many people from Britain made pilgrimages to these places and were deeply impacted. Some had huge expectations of worldwide revival. In these heady days there were many prophecies concerning revival in our land. A number of people, including leaders, felt let down because these and other movements didn't fully meet their expectations. Personally, I was deeply impacted through Toronto and do not share the perspectives of those who feel let down. Our testimony is that the life of our church has been enhanced and we are the better for what we have received. However, I do have sympathy for some whose hopes and aspirations were not met and I believe that disillusionment has contributed to some of the needs of the church today.

'Why I left the charismatic church'

During the time that I was thinking about the state of the church in Britain, a friend sent me two tapes which he thought I might be interested to hear. The tapes went under the title of, 'Why I left the Charismatic Church'. I have to confess, I left the tapes for a while because I didn't want to be depressed! I also felt I wanted to give a little space so that I could listen more objectively. Inwardly I was pretty sure I would not be surprised by the content. When I eventually listened to the tapes I heard point after point as to why the speaker had left the charismatic fold. Having listened to the reasons he gave, I felt I could have added a few more myself! I finished listening to the tapes with a sense of sadness that a number of people I hold in high esteem were mentioned by name. Later in the talk I even heard my own name mentioned as someone to be careful of. I believe we all have a right to our perspectives, and it helps sometimes to disagree, but naming people as being 'dangerous', troubled me. I have made the decision only to mention names in the context of encouragement and to try to deal with principles not personalities. I am not sure the speaker was ever a charismatic, but I was aware that he had been hurt. Some of the things he levelled at charismatics were undoubtedly true, and I think that Paul's teaching to the Christians at Corinth provides an antidote to these problems which we will examine later.

'Safe churches'

For a number of years now, many 'pioneer' ministries that emerged during the early days of the charismatic movement, have decided to go back into denominational churches. Some have retreated into the safer environment of establishment. On occasions the things they sought to change they have now embraced. The vestments they cast off have been put on again. Of course, each would have their reasons for doing so, but people who have been impacted and shaped through their example have sometimes been left bewildered. This is a major challenge to so-called new churches that have prided themselves in being on the frontline of change in the nation. The apostle Paul warned against the danger of becoming institutionalised.

Immorality

Perhaps the fall from grace of certain TV evangelists has given the impression that it is the charismatic church that have opened themselves to immorality. However the truth is that all kinds of churches of differing style and belief have been infected. The divorce rate among church leaders is growing and sadly we hear of infidelity, broken relationships and even child abuse. Many find themselves locked into various un-wholesome Internet sites and counsellors are encountering a growing level of shame within church circles. Standards are slipping and people in the media who stand for biblical values are belittled.

Defining 'charismatic'

The church at Corinth was a 'charismatic' church. This book is therefore not just referencing the charismatic movement that broke out in Britain in the late 1960s early 1970s, but a far wider constituency of churches who have embraced the work of the Spirit. I have found David Pawson's definition of 'charismatic' in his book *Fourth Wave*[1] very helpful. He speaks of two aspects that are essential. He defines charismatics as those who recognise that 'the gift of the Spirit is to be experienced, and the gifts of the Spirit are to be exercised'. This highlights the *receiving* element and the *giving* element. There are those who attend charismatic fellowships who are not really charismatic. Critics often see charismatics as self-centred people looking for the latest experience, but genuine charismatic Christianity has to do with contributing to the life and growth of the church and impacting and bringing life to those who do not yet know Christ.

So why are Paul's letters to Corinth important for today? I believe that the things outlined above have created an environment that is now waiting for answers. Our post-modern mindset makes it very difficult to address that which is wrong, but it is very clear that Paul spoke into issues at Corinth that are found in today's church. It is my conviction that the Bible has much to say that can untangle and bring clarity. Today we need leaders to emerge who know God's word and are confident about God's church.

So, on to the challenges. Corinth was a thoroughly charismatic church. They did not lack any spiritual gift (1 Corinthians 1:7) and were *'eager to have spiritual gifts'* (1 Corinthians 14:12). However, there was much that was out of order. The following lists outline the issues that Paul addresses and the teaching he brings to correct them. All these issues are prevalent in today's church in Britain. The Bible has something to speak into all these things:

▶ *The challenges*

- Cliques and personality cults (1 Corinthians 1:10–17; 3:1–22)

- Arguments and disputes (1 Corinthians 6)

- General chaos in church services, even during the Lord's Supper (1 Corinthians 11:17–22; 14:26–40)

- Immorality (1 Corinthians 5:1–12; 12–20)

- Abuse of Christian freedom (1 Corinthians 10)

▶ *Paul's teaching*
- The body of Christ
- Christian behaviour
- Communion
- Gifts of the Holy Spirit
- Marriage
- Purity of relationships
- Discipline in the church
- Servant leadership
- Christian freedom
- Propriety in worship
- Love

▶ *The two pillars*
- The cross
- The resurrection

Chapter 2

The Mess Called Church

Irene, my wife, and her good friend, Kath, suggested another title for this chapter. I modified the shock-value and decided on the above!

There is no doubt that the church in Corinth was in a real mess in many ways. It is therefore remarkable that Paul begins his first letter with words of support and affirmation. The Oxford Popular Dictionary defines 'mess' as 'a dirty or untidy condition; an untidy collection of things; a difficult and confused situation; trouble'. All of these words describe well the Corinthian church. However, it seems as though Paul looked beyond these things and saw a finished article that was very different. Some people have the ability to walk into dirty or even derelict buildings and in their mind's eye see beauty and order. Paul was such a person. He saw something and said so. He would not avoid the mess – in fact, he addresses everything that is out of order – but still he sees beyond it. What a lesson this is for the Christian community who seem to see more readily what isn't right than what is or what could be. Paul was very aware that the Christ that had apprehended him on the road to Damascus had looked beyond the terrorist he was and saw an apostle in the making, and so he extended the same grace to others. So what was it that Paul saw?

He saw a people in process

1 Corinthians 1:2 says,

> *'To the church of God in Corinth, to those sanctified in Christ Jesus and called to be holy.'*

Paul was able to recognise that the grace of God was at work. He had every confidence that what God had begun He would complete. They didn't seem to be a sanctified or holy people, but that's how Paul saw them. Eugene Peterson in his introduction to 1 Corinthians highlights an important fact. He writes, 'Conversion to Christ and His ways doesn't automatically furnish a person with impeccable manners and suitable morals.'[2] All of us are on a journey. Change and process are important. That is why teaching and fellowship are so vital.

He saw a people under protection

Though there was much to address, Paul recognised that they were 'in Christ Jesus' (1 Corinthians 1:4). God's grace was working in them; they had been enriched in every way (verse 5). He then makes one of the most remarkable statements in the whole of his letter: 'Therefore you do not lack any spiritual gift as you eagerly wait for our Lord Jesus Christ to be revealed' (verse 7). These were a people who were passionate about their faith; they had been blessed with all kinds of gifts. Paul then affirms the protective love of God in their lives: 'He will keep you strong to the end . . . ' (verse 8), and finally states with confidence that the end product will be worth waiting for ' . . . so that you will be blameless on the day of our Lord Jesus Christ' (verse 8).

However, the mess needed to be cleaned out of the way and after Paul's strong endorsement of the church in the first nine verses of 1 Corinthians 1, he swiftly moves to address the issues. As each of these issues is dealt with separately in more detail elsewhere, I will simply outline and reference the issues that needed his urgent attention:

▶ *The mess of disunity*
- 1 Corinthians 1:10–17
- 1 Corinthians 3:1–22
- 1 Corinthians 6:1–11

▶ *The mess of immorality*
- 1 Corinthians 5:1–12
- 1 Corinthians 6:12–20

▶ *The mess of disorder*

* 1 Corinthians 11:17–22
* 1 Corinthians 14:26–39

In dealing with these things head-on, Paul has provided the church with an incredible wealth of material giving positive instruction for holy living. He wants the mess removed, but majors on the alternative lifestyle that the gospel offers. For instance, in addressing division and disunity Paul brings teaching on the body of Christ, emphasising how each part needs to be connected with every other part and particularly to the head which is Christ. Again, Eugene Peterson writes, 'Paul's first letter to the Corinthians is a classic pastoral response; affectionate, firm, clear and unswerving in the conviction that God among them, revealed in Jesus and present in his Holy Spirit, continued to be the central issue in their lives, regardless of how much of a mess they had made of things.'[3]

The Church has often been perceived as being 'against' things. There is no doubt that Paul was angry with the moral state of the church, but having strongly stated his case, he moves on to bring teaching on marriage and purity. It is my conviction that the church generally needs to change its stance from consistently speaking out against things. We need to tell the world what we stand for and major on that which is good. Paul gives more attention in this letter to teaching how the church *ought* to live, than knocking that which is wrong. The mess needs clearing up, but constantly telling the church what a mess it is in will not bring change. Having addressed its mess, the church should move into a stance of support and help. This is where I would challenge some of our brothers and sisters who attack the charismatic position. They sadly argue that Corinth, which was clearly a charismatic community, was the church with the *most* mess. This gives the critics a rationale for attacking the charismatic church at large, but many then fail to endorse Paul's teaching on the gifts of the Holy Spirit in 1 Corinthians 12, which was written as a corrective word so that the gifts would be properly used; they ignore Paul's teaching, suggesting that it was only relevant to a past dispensation.

In a similar way, Paul speaks correctively into the area of 'disorder'. It is hard to imagine how wild some of the church meetings must have been. Getting drunk at the Lord's Table, then disrupting the meeting by jumping in with some spiritual utterance takes some believing. Yet, the main thrust of Paul's letter is restorative. How many of us, charismatic and non-charismatics alike, have used the wonderful words of 1 Corinthians 11 as a guideline for our communion services? He also gives teaching on the use of the gifts of the Holy Spirit in 1 Corinthians 12 – 14. Without these chapters made available to us, we would have very little information or help in overseeing Holy Spirit-filled worship and ministry. This letter should help us guard against the excesses that are outlined, but be released into the safety of its wise counsel. Strangely, the church's definition of 'decently and in order' bears very little resemblance to that which Scripture reveals. Corinth was definitely confused about where the boundaries of good order lay, but the 'playing safe' and rigid rules of some modern churches is not the order of vibrant New Testament Christianity either.

In this chapter it would be easy to give much attention to the mess that the church in Britain is now in. I guess that many people could add their strong perspectives to anything I write. However, I do think that it is appropriate to highlight some things that need attention. It is my conviction that we are living in a culture today that really resembles that of the Corinthian scene. Anyone finding faith today is likely to bring with them a lot of 'baggage' that will need sorting out. No longer do we live in a country where Christian values are known. There is generally very little knowledge of what the Bible teaches. Switch on any quiz or general knowledge programme and listen to the answers given regarding questions about the Bible. Many would not even know the name of the first book in the Bible, let alone believe in its contents.

There is no doubt that our churches are feeling the shift that has rapidly taken place. Without going into detail at this point it is clear that many churches have been infected with division, immorality and every kind of sin that is prevalent in our society. The greatest sadness of course lies in the knowledge that often the church's voice has been uncertain and compromising. Church leaders who have opportunity to speak, often project the view that the church has lost its way. However, it is worth noting here that there are some notable exceptions. Listening to Joel Edwards, the General Secretary of the Evangelical Alliance, on the panel of the BBC programme *Question Time* was refreshing. It was obvious that he was standing against the tide of the views in the studio, but received a strong endorsement through a telephone poll later. It was also good to hear James Jones, the Bishop of Liverpool, on a programme about 'Faith', standing for biblical truth.

Surely, it is time for the church to revisit its call and mission. Churches that are clear in their conviction tend to be those that are experiencing growth. Our nation needs the help and focus of churches in other parts of the world that have not compromised their stand. God bless the Nigerian church that is exploding in that nation at this present time and is speaking into part of the declining church in our nation.

Every local church has its share of mess. The mess needs addressing. Biblical Christianity needs to re-emerge. Our nation needs discipling again and we need to look beyond the mess and see the glory.

Chapter 3

Corinth –
the Place and the Culture

In order to understand Paul's letters to the Corinthians, it is important that we take some time to look at the city and its culture.

Its location

Corinth stood on the narrow neck of land connecting mainland Greece with the Southern Peninsula between the Aegean and Adriatic seas. It had a position of strategic commercial importance receiving ships from every major city of the Mediterranean. It had two harbours. Corinth became the capital of the Roman Province of Achaia and attracted people of many nationalities. It was dominated by the Acro-Corinth, a steep rock on which the Acropolis and a temple to Aphrodite (goddess of love) was built. No city in Greece was more favourably situated for land and sea trade. The shipping trade was intense and often smaller ships would be pulled overland on rollers to be re-launched for the next leg of their journey.

Its influence

Corinth was a highly influential and flourishing city. It was alive with trade and industry and was particularly well known for its ceramics. Within easy reach of Athens, it became a major centre of activity with a huge floating population. At the peak of its influence, it had a population of around 200,000 plus many slaves who were attached to its Navy.

Julius Caesar re-established Corinth in 46 BC and populated it with Roman veterans and freed men. Increasingly these freed men, who were ordinary people, began to prosper within the city. There was often strong rivalry between Corinth and the university town of Athens, and Corinth emerged with an interesting blend of both Roman and Greek thinking. Someone has said of Corinth that, 'In every street you met a "wise man".' Acts 18 introduces us to the setting for Paul's letters. Having left Athens, Paul makes contact with the Jewish community in Corinth. Inscriptions found show that the synagogue was unimpressive and the Jewish community was struggling. In fact, Sosthenes, the synagogue ruler, was beaten as a result of his contact with Paul (Acts 18:17). So, in the natural, Corinth was a place of merging ideas. The Greeks, Romans and Jews all influenced the shaping of Corinthian culture.

Paul would have walked the Lechaeum Road, passed the Greek Baths and been in the crowds who shopped at the Forum. He would have visited the Macellum, or meat market (1 Corinthians 10:25), and seen the Temple of Apollo. Located near the centre of the Market Place was the 'Bema' (Acts 18:12) – the judicial bench. There were also many temples and shrines. The city had two theatres, one of which seated 18,000 people. In a paved street east of this theatre a re-used paving block was found with the inscription, 'Erastus, the Aedile (Commissioner of Public Works), bore the expenses of this pavement'. Did this man become one of Paul's fellow workers (Acts 19:22; Romans 16:23)? The city was also host to the Isthmian games. Often runners competed naked because the human body was being celebrated. So, Corinth was a hive of activity.

The culture

What was it that made the city tick? What were the main influences that shaped Corinth? There is no doubt that, though Corinth was an exciting city, it was a city with many social, moral and spiritual problems. Some understanding of these things will help shed light on Paul's letters to the church at Corinth. In 1 Corinthians 6:9–10 Paul mentions a number of the sins that are prevalent in the city. They include sexual immorality, idolatry and drunkenness. In the following verse he states, *'And that is what some of you were'* (verse 11).

Immorality

Corinth was a typical seaport, which led to sexual permissiveness. Overshadowing the city stood the Temple to Aphrodite where it was estimated that more than 1,000 female prostitutes operated. The Greek language developed the word *korinthiazomai*, which meant, 'to live like a Corinthian in the practice of sexual immorality'. Imagine living in Corinth – the very name of the city suggested you could be infected. To 'Corinthianise' became a byword for excess and sexual licence.

Idolatry

The city was filled with shrines and temples. Much of the meat sold in the busy market area had been offered to idols. There must have been a strong sense that things had been tainted by the many religions and false gods that vied for position and prominence.

Drunkenness

According to the *NIV Bible Commentary* Volume 2, 'Around the market were a good many shops, numbers of which had individual wells, suggesting that much wine was made and drunk in the city'[4] (hence Paul's warning in 1 Corinthians 6:10). With the combination of many sailors killing time in town, high levels of prostitution, and easily available alcohol, it is not difficult to imagine the nightlife of Corinth.

More subtle influences

Many of the issues in Corinth were prominent and visible, but other pitfalls were less obvious. Though Corinth was a Greek city, it enjoyed Roman law and order. Although this was not necessarily a bad thing in itself, Corinth was a city struggling for identity. Some new believers in the church had embraced the Roman law and taken it too far, ending in them taking fellow believers to court (1 Corinthians 6).

There was also the strong influence of Greek philosophy. The word 'democracy' is of Greek origin and was working its way into the church. The freethinking individuals demanded their say and Paul has his work cut out when trying to bring some order to the believers.

The Corinthian way of thinking also meant there was often a separation between the *physical* and the *spiritual*. (Incidentally, the Western church today still tends to have boxes marked 'secular' and 'sacred'.) The Greeks believed that the body was not integral to the soul. In Hebrew thought, the body was very important. But bodies being 'temples of the Holy Spirit' was a concept not easily understood by the Corinthian mind. With this background we can begin to understand why Paul took so much time emphasising the importance of the physical, bodily resurrection of Jesus. These Greek thought patterns led to extremes with regard to physical bodies. Within Corinth, either bodies were undervalued through immoral acts, or were celebrated in 'the Games' and given inappropriately high recognition.

The culture of Corinth in Paul's day was very similar to today's British scene. We are living in an increasingly spiritual 'pick-and-mix' environment where people take a little from a variety different religions and philosophies. Hence the clear teaching of biblical values is essential. In Corinth the inhabitants worshipped the gods of Greece and Rome including Poseidon, god of the sea, and Aphrodite, goddess of love. Paul knew that in order to evangelise Corinth the church had to be different. It was essential that the church should affect the city, rather than the city affect the church. In the words of G. Campbell-Morgan, 'What the church supremely needs is to correct the spirit of the age. The church in Corinth, catching the spirit of Corinth became anaemic, weak and unable to deliver the message of God to Corinth.'[5] The church in Britain can only make a difference by being different and living according to God's pattern. A vibrant holy church could change the strategic city of Corinth, and equally, so can it change the cities of our world today.

> In a time of change
>   as a new day's dawning
>   my hope is built on You.

As nations rise
  against each other
  my hope is built on You.

Do we trust in You enough Lord?
Is our faith in things unseen?
Forgive us of impatience.
Keep us running with these dreams.

It's all about You Jesus.
Nothing I do can ever replace Your love.
I'll stand by Your truth my Jesus
  'cause the hope for this world
  is found in You

As creation groans
  and cities crumble
  my hope is built on You.
When children flee
  from desperate struggles
  my hope is built on You.

Chapter 4

Spirit-filled but Divided?

When the Spirit comes, one would expect the marks of the Spirit to be evidenced in behaviour. However, as has already been mentioned, there is a big difference between *charisma* and *character*. It is possible for new believers to be quickly filled with the Holy Spirit, but the fruit of the Spirit takes time to develop and grow.

Gifted but divided

The church at Corinth was highly gifted but greatly divided. This is one of the saddest truths that the church has to live with today. Disunity was robbing the church of its potential, ruining its witness and bringing discredit to its Master. It is hard to imagine how the church at Corinth could be so gifted and yet so immature. In 1 Corinthians 1:7 Paul affirms their giftedness, *'Therefore you do not lack any spiritual gift as you eagerly wait for Jesus Christ to be revealed.'* He later speaks of their eagerness for spiritual gifts (1 Corinthians 14:12) and yet they are incredibly divided.

Paul addresses division

Throughout his letters Paul persistently battles for unity. He 'appeals to the church' in 1 Corinthians 1:10. This is translated 'I beg' in the *New Century Bible*.[6] It is very evident that this is a major issue for Paul. His strength of argument and word choice underlines the urgency of his appeal, *'I appeal to you, brothers, in the name of our Lord Jesus Christ, that all of you agree with one another so that there may be no divisions among*

you and that you may be perfectly united in mind and thought.'
Some have argued that charismatic churches cause divisions.
It is important to note that Paul endorses the charismatic
element, but addresses the problems. In chapter 3:1 Paul
states, *'Brothers I could not address you as spiritual but as worldly
– mere infants in Christ.'*

The issue was one of immaturity. This worldliness needs
challenging in the church today. The Corinthians' church was
meant to walk in unity. It was not enough that they moved in
spiritual gifts, they needed to grow up and exhibit, not only
the gifts, but also the fruit of the Spirit. John Stott writes, 'The
unity of the church is as indestructible as the unity of God
Himself. It is no more possible to split the church than it is
possible to split the Godhead.'[7]

Personality cults

The church at Corinth was filled with disagreements and
quarrelling. People lined up behind their favourite ministries
only giving their support to those they liked, or at best those
who suited them. Instead of gladly recognising the variety of
ministries and gifts that God had given to them, they formed
their own particular cliques. They chose leaders like choosing
politicians. You can be sure that self-interest was at the root of
their actions. Different groups emerged, no doubt with self-
appointed antagonists who were looking for power and
influence among the group of likeminded people.

In church life we will always have our preferences. The
reality is we have our favourite speakers or worship leaders,
but maturing people learn to receive from all of God's gifts
and give honour where honour is due. If we love God we will
love those He gives to us.

Paul recognises that there are at least four factions in the
church at Corinth. He also had to give wise advice as one of
the groups supported Paul himself. If Paul had been insecure
or had personal agendas, he could have used this knowledge
as an opportunity for power and influence, a thing that he
refused to do. A cell group at Chloe's house (1 Corinthians
1:11) gave Paul information with regard to the developing
factions that were causing damage to the church. The four
groups could be summarised as follows:

1. **The founders' group**
   These were the people who rallied around Paul. Their
   calling card was 'I follow Paul' (verse 12). No doubt, today
   they would be wearing his T-shirt. This was not so much
   an affirmation of Paul, but a statement that they didn't
   much like the rest of the ministry team.

2. **The thinkers' group**
   Apollos was the rallying point for this group. Unknown
   to him, his ministry was being lifted up as 'the best'. He
   was the radical thinker, less heavy than Paul, and a great
   speaker. Perhaps he told more jokes and had a pioneering
   spirit. He certainly was a sharp communicator and in
   great demand throughout the network of churches.

3. **The traditional group**
   There were those in the church who felt far more secure
   when Peter (Cephas) was around. These people no doubt
   saw the apostle to the Jews as rooted in the traditions of
   the early mother church of Jerusalem. When he was
   around, the Jewish flavour came through strongly. Paul's
   style, out of necessity, embraced a Gentile approach to
   things and for this group Apollos was no doubt far too
   radical. We can only imagine how these different factions
   supported their particular corner. Each group became
   increasingly inflexible and un-teachable, yet another sign
   of immaturity. Does all this sound familiar? Oh no,
   they're not leading worship this week are they? Oh, so
   and so is speaking today – boring! 'Please bring back Jeff
   Lucas', I hear you cry!

4. **The exclusive group**
   Known to some as the 'super-spirituals', this group was
   perhaps the worst of all. They would smugly say, 'I follow
   Christ' (1 Corinthians 1:12), the inference being that they
   were directly under the leadership of Jesus. Of course this
   is how *all* Christians ought to be. However, this was a
   stance that in reality was saying, 'I don't need to listen to
   you.' This group cannot be reasoned with, counselled or
   easily advised because they are likely to simply smile and
   say, 'God told me.' Don't misunderstand me, my hope is

that all of us can hear from God for ourselves, but 'exclusive' and 'fellowship' are two words that don't easily go together. We were designed to be part of a body. Paul develops this theme later in his letters giving many verses to the subject of the body of Christ. Every member is important and every part unique. Instead of choosing our favourite ministries we are called on to recognise and receive all the gifted people that God has graciously given us. In 1 Corinthians 3:21–23 Paul asserts, *'So then no more boasting about men, all things are yours, whether Paul or Apollos or Cephas or the world or life or death or the present or the future – all are yours and you are of Christ, and Christ is of God.'* Why would we want just a part when in Christ we can enjoy the lot?

One body – many parts

There are two phrases that Paul uses in 1 Corinthians 12 that highlight two important issues. The first is found in 1 Corinthians 12:16: *'Because I am not . . . '* Expanded it reads, *'Because I am not an eye, I do not belong to the body . . . '* One could replace the word 'eye' with a host of other reasons that people put forward for not being committed to being a part of the body of Christ: 'Because I am not . . . spiritual enough . . . gifted . . . wise . . . a good person . . . ' etc. Typically people will look at others in the church whom they perceive to have 'wonderful' gifts, assuming that their own gift is inferior. Most of us at some time are tempted with these thoughts. However, Paul says, *' . . . it would not for that reason cease to be a part of the body.'* All of us have our place.

The second phrase is found in verse 21: *' . . . I don't need you!'* In context: *'The eye cannot say to the hand, "I don't need you!"'* Paul teaches that no one can rightly say that he has no need of other parts of the body. Nobody has all the gifts. The body is designed in such a way that we all need to be fitted together and joined with every other part. As Paul humorously says, *'If the whole body were an ear where would the sense of smell be?'* (1 Corinthians 12:17). Every human body is more than an ear or a nose and the same is true of the church. So the truth is, *'Now you are the body of Christ, and each one of you is a part of it'* (1 Corinthians 12:27).

Characteristics of charismatic leadership

We have looked at people's attitudes and responses to church leadership. We will now look at the leaders themselves. As we know, leaders of churches can also exhibit insecurity. Leadership teams may theologically believe in the plurality of ministries, but nobody is beyond the possibility of hidden agendas of ambition and self-interest. Paul highlights three things that would help leaders to be the kind of people who would gain the respect of those who give them the gift of leadership.

Attitude

In using the examples of leaders who have had input into the church at Corinth, Paul makes it clear that all leadership needs the right attitude. In 1 Corinthians 3:5 he asks the question, *'What, after all, is Apollos? And what is Paul?'* In answering the question Paul does not present us with a CV of ministry credentials or a newsletter of foreign travels, but gives the simple answer, *'Only servants through whom you came to believe.'* What a refreshingly simple answer. For genuine charismatic leaders these words are liberating. They remove the pressure from our shoulders and ought to release us to serve His people. Other verses in Paul's letters reveal that this is not without God-given authority, but the bottom line is that we are all called to serve.

Assignment

Paul completes his answer to the question with the words, *'. . . as the Lord has assigned to each his task'* (1 Corinthians 3:5). This is a releasing thought. If we stick to our assignment and are content to be who we are called to be, we will find fulfilment. It is when we try to be like someone else or do things which we are not called to do that we get into difficulties. So often leaders appear to be striving for greater visibility or prominence. It is frustrating to always be looking for more, but it is a fulfilling thing to be content in an assigned place. Some are called to planting, others to watering, but ultimately it is God who makes things grow.

Acceptance

Paul makes it clear that we are called to work *together*. We need to accept other ministries and gifts. A friend of mine has coined the phrase, 'Your success is my honour.' When competition is removed and we recognise that there really is only one body, we grow in maturity. We begin to value every ministry and gift. They actually become 'ours'. What a great place the church of Jesus really is. There are so many gifts displaying God's multi-coloured grace.

Spiritual or worldly?

In 1 Corinthians 3 we see the depths to which Christians can fall. Worldly Christians can only really cope with milk. This picture painted by Paul reveals the infantile attitudes of the Corinthian church. It will eventually need to eat meat and grow up. At present it is marked out by jealousy and quarrelling, yet God wants it to move from being worldly to being spiritual. Paul then looks to the future and we get a view of the heights to which believers can rise. In verse 9 we catch a glimpse of the mature community, *'For we are God's fellow workers; you are God's field, God's building.'* In verse 16 Paul asks, *'Don't you know that you yourselves are God's temple and that God's Spirit lives in you?'* In chapter 6 he even sees their future destiny – a people walking in maturity who are called to bring wise judgement not only to the church and the world, but also to angels (chapter 6:2–3).

> God of grace,
> I turn my face to You,
> I cannot hide;
> My nakedness, my shame, my guilt, are all before Your
>   eyes.
> Striving and all anguished dreams in rags lie at my feet;
> And only grace provides the way for me to stand
>   complete.
>
> And Your grace clothes me in righteousness,
> And Your mercy covers me in love.
> Your life adorns and beautifies,
> I stand complete in You.
>
> (Chris Bowater. Copyright © 1990,
> Sovereign Lifestyle Music Ltd, PO Box 356,
> Leighton Buzzard, LU7 3WP, UK.
> Reproduced by permission.)

Chapter 5

In the Light of the Cross

The place of the cross

I find it interesting how Paul structures his first letter to the Corinthian church. After affirming the church in the first section of chapter 1, he immediately addresses the issue of broken relationships. He then brings teaching on the cross before returning to the problems of division in chapter 3. This is no accident. Paul clearly places the cross *between* the divisions in the church. The cross is lifted as a pillar of doctrine against a backdrop of division, immorality and worldliness. The arms of the crucified Christ were always extended between the factions and divisions of the world. In the cross, Jews and Gentiles, male and female, black and white, find unity. In the cross, the deepest chasms of division and brokenness can find an answer. So, at the very beginning of this letter, the first pillar of doctrine is lifted high bringing stability, wholeness and purity. In the light of this teaching the destiny for God's people in Corinth is secured. At the end of the letter a second pillar of truth is erected. This is the resurrection of Christ. Chapter 15 that contains 55 verses is given to this important doctrine. In fact, this is the most detailed of all Paul's writings on this subject. We will pick up on the importance of the bodily resurrection of Jesus in the following chapter, but the cross (at the beginning of the letter) and the resurrection (at the end of the letter) bring stability, healing and life into the brokenness and impurity of the church. These two pillars are connected, foundational truths which are essential for all churches and for all time. Bob Gordon writes, 'The essence of the cross is made good in us through the power of the resurrection.'[8] Time and again the New Testament affirms this link.

Paul, with razor-sharp clarity, gets straight into the message of the cross. There are no complicated words. Corinth was filled with all kinds of fancy ideas and every street was awash with philosophy. People are not saved by what they know, but who they know. Paul declares confidently, *'But we preach Christ crucified'* (1 Corinthians 1:23). His focus is simple and clear, *'For I resolved to know nothing while I was with you except Jesus Christ and Him crucified'* (1 Corinthians 2:2). The Greeks were constantly looking for wisdom. Philosophers like Plato and Aristotle used the cleverness of human argument, but Paul wants the cross to speak for itself. Paul could match the best in debate, but here he chooses not the way of human argument, but confidently points to the truth of the cross. Paul even felt that if he were to fall into the trap of speaking clever words that he could empty the cross of its power. His calling was to preach the gospel, *'. . . not with words of human wisdom, lest the cross of Christ be emptied of its power'* (1 Corinthians 1:17).

The preaching of this message produced two effects: *'The message of the cross is **foolishness** to those who are perishing, but to us who are being saved it is **the power of God'*** (1 Corinthians 1:18). The preaching of the cross always demands a choice. To the Jewish people the cross became a stumbling block. This was because they were looking for miraculous signs. They were bent on seeing a Messiah emerge who would break the power of Roman oppression, but they could not easily embrace the notion that a man dying on a cross could be their deliverer. Even though their scriptures depicted a suffering servant, they were not easily convinced that the Christ would actually die, especially on a cross that carried the stigma of curse with it.

On the other hand, for the Greeks the whole message seemed utterly foolish. How could a cross, used for killing criminals, provide salvation? They thought that through wisdom they would discover the answers to life, so a thorn-crowned dying man made no sense at all. *'Jews demand miraculous signs and Greeks look for wisdom, but we preach Christ crucified: a stumbling block to Jews and foolishness to Gentiles'* (1 Corinthians 1:22–23).

The message of the cross still stands as God's answer for all people, no matter where they live or when they live. Through the centuries of church history, the cross has opened up the way back to God for millions. All people and cultures meet God here. We may package the message differently at different times and for different people groups, but ultimately at the cross the justice and love of God perfectly meet, putting fallen humanity back into relationship with their Creator once again. Amazingly, the very thing the Jews were looking for was found in the cross. Incredibly this was the very power of God released. Talk about a sign or a wonder! This was God in Christ smashing the power of sin, death and hell, and rattling open the bars of the prison to set the captives free.

The cross also answered the Greeks desire for wisdom. Who could have ever conceived such a wonderful plan that God would die that we might live. When we really see what Christ has done for us and the blindfolds are removed from our eyes, we find ourselves wanting to cling to the old rugged cross, for it is here that we first saw the light and the burden of our heart rolled away. *'To those whom God has called, both Jews and Greeks, Christ the power of God and the wisdom of God'* (1 Corinthians 1:24).

The power of the cross

Paul sees himself as a weak messenger with a strong message. He says, *'I came to you in weakness and fear, and with much trembling'* (1 Corinthians 2:3). The cross did not impress the Jews and the Greeks could not understand the cross, but Paul declares the power of the cross. He says, *'To us who are being saved it is the power of God'* (1 Corinthians 1:18). Paul opted not to bring persuasive words, but believed that as the cross was preached its power would be evidenced, *'with a demonstration of the Spirit's power'* (1 Corinthians 2:4). He believed that as the cross was preached, power would be released to the church. He expected that this doctrine would transform the Corinthian church. In the light of the cross things change, battles stop, vying for position is no longer an option and competitive factions become an insult. This message will reshape the church, but it will also affect the city. The cross, when preached on the streets of Corinth, would begin to change it.

Any individual who trusted in the finished work of Christ would become a new creation. In another of his letters Paul's writes, *'I am not ashamed of the gospel, because it is the power of God for the salvation of everyone who believes: first for the Jew then for the Gentile'* (Romans 1:16).

> If it wasn't for the blood I'd be dead;
> If it wasn't for the blood I'd be hopeless;
> If it wasn't for the blood I'd be lost;
> If it wasn't for the blood of my ...
>
> *Jesus ... Saviour ... Reconciler*
> *Only ... Way back ... to the Father.*
>
> If it wasn't for the blood I'd be blamed;
> If it wasn't for the blood I'd be guilty;
> If it wasn't for the blood I'd be vile;
> If it wasn't for the blood
> If it wasn't for the blood of my ...
>
> I come to the cross, where I'm set free;
> Foolishness to some,
> But the power of God to me ...
>
> (Godfrey Birtill, Whitefield Music UK,
Admin. Copycare, © 1999)

Chapter 6

The Resurrection Is for Real

In this chapter we move on to look at the second essential doctrinal pillar which Paul seeks to place between the problems of broken relationship and division, namely, the resurrection of Christ. It comes right at the end of his letter, sandwiching with the doctrine of the cross, all the problems within the Corinthian church. This gives perspective. In fact the problems are seen for what they are when held against such grand confessions of faith. The resurrection is a fundamental doctrine of the faith. It is an essential part of the gospel and is as Paul declares *'of first importance'* (chapter 15:3), together with the death and burial of Jesus. 'The resurrection of Christ concentrates the whole of salvation into a single event. It is the turning point of the ages and the centre of time. Henceforth not only time but life itself can never be the same.'[9]

The Corinthians were surrounded by Greek ideas and concepts with regard to physical and spiritual issues. Paul clearly argues that the resurrection did not take place in the minds of the disciples, but was a real and witnessed event. In a world of ideas and shifting arguments, he sets about with forensic detail, arguing that Christ physically rose from the dead. People saw Jesus before and after the event. The clear evidence for the resurrection, when examined with an open mind, is convincing. Wayne Grudem writes, 'The historical arguments for the resurrection of Christ are substantial and have persuaded many sceptics who started to examine the evidence for the purpose of disproving the resurrection.[10] The best known account of such a change from scepticism to belief is Frank Morrison's book, *Who Moved the Stone?* '[11]

The weight of witnesses

Paul brings an impressive list of witnesses to the resurrection, starting with Peter (Cephas) and the twelve disciples (1 Corinthians 15:5–6). *'After that, he appeared to more than five hundred of the brothers at the same time, most of whom are still living, though some have fallen asleep'* (1 Corinthians 15:6). Just imagine! Many eyewitnesses could still be interviewed. I guess many churches would have testimony times with visitors who would say, 'I was there, lots of us saw him at the same time.' Paul then states that James was also a witness. Everyone believed James: he was a dependable pillar in the church. Finally, Paul includes himself in the list and though he felt he had to wait for the revelation, his road to Damascus confrontation with Christ had totally changed the direction of his life (1 Corinthians 15:8). The church persecutor had now become the church planter.

Resurrection hope

Paul re-emphasises the importance of the bodily resurrection of Jesus. The implications, not only to the Corinthians, but to the entire world are far reaching. So much hinges on whether the resurrection is for real. Paul brings three arguments:

1. If there is no resurrection then Christ can't have been raised (verse 13). If witnesses had been misled or deceived then the church would have no viable message. The teachings of Christ would have no validity and there would be no clear foundations for meaningful faith.

2. If Christ is not raised, we will not be raised. This means that life is futile and faith lacks power; the church is robbed of hope and there is no good news to proclaim. Preaching has no power and daily Christian living becomes meaningless.

3. If Christ is not raised, we are still held captive to the eternal consequences of our sins (verses 17–18). The human condition of 'fallenness' remains. There is no solution, therefore there is no gospel. The doctrine of the resurrection really is the hinge that opens the door

into God's presence and promises a new day, when the decaying old order of things is done away with.

At this point, when reading the letter, you can almost hear Paul raise his voice and proclaim with certainty one word: *But ...!* This word makes a difference for the whole of humanity. *'But Christ has indeed been raised from the dead'* (1 Corinthians 15:20). This is the certainty of the Christian faith and that which marks it out as different from any other religion.

Two men

Paul develops his arguments through two men, Adam, the first man, and Christ, the last Adam (1 Corinthians 15:45). The fall of the first man was so severe that paradise was lost. Decay entered the world and the law of sin and death began to rule. What was needed was a second man of a completely different order. Jesus stepped into the world both as perfect man and perfect God. He perfectly met the requirements of His holy Father and destroyed the power of death that had held humanity in bondage. As death came through the first Adam, so life comes through Jesus. The following lists summarise the consequences of the lives of both Adam and Jesus:

Adam	**Christ**
Death (verse 21)	Resurrection (verse 21)
All die (verse 22)	All made alive (verse 22)
Living being (verse 45)	Life-giving spirit (verse 45)
From dust (verse 47)	From heaven (verse 47)
Likeness of earthly man (verse 49)	Likeness of man from heaven (verse 49)

Death	**Resurrection**
Perishable (verse 42)	Imperishable (verse 42)
Dishonour (verse 43)	Glory (verse 43)
Weakness (verse 43)	Power (verse 43)
Natural (verse 44)	Spiritual (verse 44)

Everything that was lost through Adam's rebellion has been retrieved through Christ. The downward pull of the fall leading to death and destruction has been replaced by an upward move from dust to glory. To be in Christ is to be secure. Flesh and blood cannot inherit the kingdom of God, but the truth is we will all be changed and ultimately will exchange these earthly bodies for bodies that are more suitable for the eternal adventure that is yet to come. In the meantime, Paul offers good advice:

> *'Therefore, my dear brothers, stand firm. Let nothing move you. Always give yourselves fully to the work of the Lord, because you know that your labour in the Lord is not in vain.'*
> (1 Corinthians 15:58)

Where is your sting, O death?
Where are your threats, O grave?
Swallowed up in victory
by the Prince of life who saves.

Death couldn't hold Him down
The stone had to roll away.
Hail now the conqueror.
Hail His resurrection day!

Now Your power has set me free,
Now Your blood has made me clean.
You have made our heart sing.
Hallelujah! Hallelujah!
He has risen! He has risen!
In anthems of praise, He is exalted now.

Now God has raised Him up
Seated in majesty
Reigning for evermore
Clothed in immortality.

Let every tongue confess
Jesus is Lord of all
His justice knows no end
His Kingdom shall never fall.

(Dave Middleton. Copyright © 2004)

Chapter 7

Our Future Confidence

(2 Corinthians 5:1–10)

Having established that all our problems are dealt with through the two great doctrinal pillars of the cross and the resurrection of Christ, in his second letter Paul moves on to address further vital issues that will help the Christians at Corinth go beyond their factions and disunity. He does this by encouraging them to take their eyes off the temporal and focus on the eternal. I chose to focus on these truths in this chapter because, as Paul knew, grasping them will inevitably change our behaviour; and if as individuals we are transformed by the truth, then so will our churches be transformed.

2 Corinthians chapter 5 relates to the previous chapter which examined the pressures of living the Christian life. Paul concluded that chapter with the words, *'For what is seen is temporary, but what is unseen is eternal.'* He picks up on the reality of the unseen world and highlights three reasons why we should have confidence in our hope in Christ:

▶ *1. Future possession of a spiritual body*
Paul has already stated in 1 Corinthians 15 that the resurrection is for real. In 2 Corinthians 5:1 he immediately lifts the reader above earthly afflictions and troubles and points them to a heavenly hope. He also draws a comparison between our earthy and 'heavenly' bodies – the transient (pictured by a tent) and the eternal (pictured by the more substantial 'house' in heaven). The flimsy image of a tent is replaced by a secure building from God. Death is seen as breaking camp in order to return home. Paul, the tent maker,

knows only too well of the nature of the tent. Though a good tent could stand up to strong winds, it was never designed to offer the security of a building with strong foundations. In fact the tent was light, easily moved and more suited to short-term occupation. The 'if' of verse 1 suggests that not everyone will die; Paul seems to think that there will be some who are alive at Christ's return. For both groups of people there will be a movement from a temporary tent to an eternal house. Against a backdrop of trouble and persecution this certainly brings a sense of confidence and hope. It is the 'here and now' that offers the challenges.

When Adam and Eve turned against God in the garden they quickly recognised their nakedness. It may well be that the glory covering them was lifted through their act of rebellion, leaving them vulnerable and hurting. Paul likens the present struggles to a longing to be 'clothed' again with heavenly garments for the regaining of paradise: *'Meanwhile we groan, longing to be clothed with our heavenly dwelling'* (2 Corinthians 5:2). There is an ache in the heart of every believer to be brought into the fullness of all that God has planned for them. In this body (tent) we long for more. In fact, *'what is mortal'* will one day be *'swallowed up by life'* (verse 5) suggesting that true life is eternal. We have eternal life now, we just need more appropriate packaging in the future. Until then, there is a spiritual groaning in the church while we wait for bodies perfectly adapted to the ecology of heaven. These thoughts remind me of the words of Jesus in Mark 14:58, *'I will destroy this man-made temple and in three days will build another, not made by man.'* Our future confidence is not some disembodied immortality, but physical resurrection. For more detail on spiritual bodies it is well worth looking at 1 Corinthians 15:35–58. *'But God gives it a body as he has determined, and to each kind of seed he gives its own body'* (verse 38).

▶ *2. Present possession of the Holy Spirit*
We have confidence for the future because God has given us His Holy Spirit as a pledge of ultimate transformation. *'Now it is God who has made us for this very purpose and has given us the Spirit as a deposit, guaranteeing what is to come'* (2 Corinthians 5:5). What a fantastic reality! We are not dealing here with vague possibilities for the future, but with something that is

guaranteed by God Himself. Notice that the next verses are filled with confidence: *'Therefore we are always confident ...'* (verse 6) and *'We are confident, I say ...'* (verse 8). When the Holy Spirit comes there are always new levels of confidence. Cowardly disciples become bold, the weak become strong, and silent followers become vibrant witnesses. The same Holy Spirit who gives us power now also brings us confidence and hope for the future.

▶ 3. Future departure into Christ's immediate presence

We remain confident that when we die we will be ushered into the immediate presence of God. In fact, just as the children of Israel had to dismantle their tents in order to march into the Promised Land, so our earthly bodies need to give way for us to find our residence with the Lord. *'Therefore we are always confident and know that as long as we are at home in the body, we are away from the Lord'* (2 Corinthians 5:6). We are living in limited dwellings seeking to *'live by faith, not by sight'* (verse 7). But a day will come when we are *'away from the body and at home with the Lord'* (verse 8). Paul preferred this option, but also wanted to make the most of every opportunity while on earth.

There will not only be a change of location in the days ahead, but also a greater level of intimacy *'with the Lord'* (verse 8). I can only imagine what that day will be like. Quite how we will respond I don't know, but one thing is certain, we will not just have a passing glance of the Lord on our grand arrival but we will be *with Him* forever. Incidentally, when we see Him, the old body with its flaws, sicknesses and inadequacies will already have been replaced. At this point you will notice that there will be no aches, pains or defects and all tears will have been dried.

These truths should affect our behaviour. Paul says, *'So we make it our goal to please him, whether we are at home in the body or away from it'* (verse 9). We need to live life to the full and walk in a way that will honour our Lord. Pleasing Him, should be our first priority and receiving His approval, our goal. What a need there is today for such responsible living. The reason that such an approach to life is imperative, Paul says, is because *'... we must appear before the judgement seat of*

Christ, that each one may receive what is due to him for the things done while in the body, whether good or bad' (verse 10). It is a sobering thought to realise that God knows everything we get up to in our tents. For most of us there is a healthy fear of God that keeps us in line. The liberating truth for believers is the fact that we don't stand condemned; we are totally accepted and freely loved. In Corinth the 'Bema' (Judgement Seat) of the city is still visible today. It is a large, richly-decorated rostrum where rewards and punishments were historically distributed. For believers, the 'Bema' is not to do with eternal destiny. The shed blood of His Son who paid the price on our behalf determined our place in God's presence. I believe that Christians are judged in respect of their stewardship of talents, gifts, opportunities and respon-sibilities. This is a fatherly judgement. 1 Peter 1:17 says, *'Since you call on a father who judges each man's work impartially, live your lives as strangers here in reverent fear.'* Appearance before Christ's tribunal is our privilege.

Our future is bright. We have read the end of the book! We need to live confidently every day to the full, knowing that the Holy Spirit is with us. A new spiritual body awaits us and one day we will be in Father's presence forever. If together we live our lives in the knowledge of this reality, we will experience new levels of unity in our churches and a new vitality in our faith.

> Glorious King,
> Seated on the highest place,
> Given the name above all names,
> Glorious King,
> Glorious King,
> Worthy of the highest praise,
> Giver of eternal days,
> Glorious King,
> Glorious King.
>
> [*Chorus*]
> *And we come, and bow,*
> *We come and bow,*
> *We come and bow before our King*
> *Our Glorious King.*

Glorious King,
All the earth declares Your praise,
Speaks the glories of Your name,
Glorious King,
Glorious King,
All creation joins in song,
Lifting up their voice as one,
Glorious King,
Glorious King.

Glorious King,
All the nations bow in awe,
Every king and priest will fall
To their knees,
Glorious King,
On that day Your truth will reign,

We'll sing the glories of Your name,
Glorious King,
Glorious King.

Chapter 8

A Clean House

After studying Paul's teaching on the cross and resurrection, it makes sense for us to give some time to the whole issue of purity among God's people. Paul has already addressed the problems of division and quarrelling and now he confronts a major issue in the church. In chapter 5 he highlights an issue of sexual immorality which the leadership at Corinth were not adequately addressing. A member of the church was sleeping with his stepmother. The word used is *porneia* meaning 'sexual immorality' or 'illicit sexual intercourse'. In this case it was incest. This was explicitly forbidden in Leviticus 18:8 and Deuteronomy 22:30 and actually carried a curse (Deuteronomy 27:20). Shocked by this information, Paul recognises that even pagans frowned upon this kind of behaviour. The church had become infected, but nothing was being done about it. Even small impurities affect churches, but this was like a boil that needed lancing. The congregation seemed to be complacent and indifferent. They should have been grieving, but they were acting as though there wasn't really a problem. We don't know why this was. Were they afraid to confront things or had they become desensitised to the seriousness of the offence?

How relevant this is in today's church. We live in days of changing attitudes towards holiness and personal moral purity. The general attitude that surrounds us suggests that everyone should be free to make up their own minds and set their own boundaries. A leadership that speaks out against impurity can soon be viewed as being out of touch or even be accused of imposing outmoded rules of behaviour on the people they care for. Leaders can then become fearful of confrontation and let problems be swept under the carpet. Paul makes it clear that the house needs to be clean underneath and on top of the carpets. The Bible remains our guideline, and increasingly so as our churches are being infected by immorality at all levels. Our daily papers regularly carry stories of moral falls and the more influential the ministry the more damaging the consequences. Breakdown of family relationships, the invading of minds through Internet pornography, and the gradual eroding of moral standards all lead to a highly complex situation.

Questions regarding marriage

This led to the leadership at Corinth asking questions of Paul. We need to understand that, in his response, Paul is not spelling out a complete theology of purity or of marriage. In 1 Corinthians 7 Paul writes in detail on these issues, but this teaching also needs to be seen alongside the rest of the Bible. The quoting of 'proof texts' doesn't do this subject justice. Some liberal critics have accused Paul of being against both marriage and women. These accusations are unfounded.

One question the leaders obviously asked Paul was to do with whether celibacy was more spiritual than marriage. Paul states that celibacy is a valid calling, but no more valid than being married. Dr Kenneth Wuest translates Paul's reply, 'It is perfectly proper, honourable, morally befitting for a man to live in strict celibacy.'[12] In today's culture singleness and celibacy are sometimes seen to be less acceptable than marriage or cohabitation.

Another highly relevant issue that Paul addresses is that of Christians who are married to non-Christians. Warren Wiersbe in his commentary on 1 Corinthians writes, 'If a person becomes a Christian after marriage, he should not use that as an excuse to break up the marriage just to avoid problems.'[13] Paul emphasises the positive position of seeking to see a marriage partner saved. It is far better to view the situation as an opportunity to be a spiritual influence for good. All too often today's people who have become Christians after marriage opt out of their responsibilities on the basis of their partner being unsaved. Paul also gives practical advice when an unconverted partner pulls away from their partner because of their Christian faith.

Another question being asked by the Corinthian church was, 'Must a Christian get married?' In answering this question the prevailing situation was taken into account by Paul. The church was being persecuted and often Christians were working within economic restraints and pressures due to their faith. Their changing world was causing much distress (1 Corinthians 7:26–31). In view of these difficulties Paul was counselling that it would be better for a person to remain unmarried. However, this did not mean that married people should consider divorce (verse 27). He was not against marriage, but those who married needed to be aware that they would face trials as a result (verse 28). The issue was with regard to entering into marriage with a measure of maturity. He was also conscious that if God's kingdom was to expand in such troubled days there would need to be focus and singleness of heart.

Avoiding moral traps

Since one of the main accusations levelled at the charismatic church is having low moral standards and a liberal approach to purity, it is all the more vital that we live according to a high moral code and avoid falling into 'moral traps'. We must use our common sense and conduct ourselves in a way that doesn't invite trouble.

Dave Gilpin, in his book *Top 10 of Everything*[14] includes a very helpful list called, 'Top 10 ways for a leader to avoid having an affair'. Despite the fact that it is aimed at those in leadership, there are principles here that will help us all.

1. **Keep on the front line**
   David fell not because he was an adulterer, but because he wasn't with the troops when he should have been. Always be on the front line of God's progressive vision for your life.

2. **Keep on the same tracks**
   If you're attracted to someone of the opposite sex, don't go out of your way to foster the relationship. Keep doing what you usually do.

3. **Keep your mind on the job**
Don't allow your mind to fantasise about anyone you're attracted to. Keep your meditation pure and focused on God's will for your life.

4. **Keep your mouth in check**
Don't share the details of personal problems between you and your partner with someone of the opposite sex. Don't allow a potential wedge to be placed between you and your ordained relationship. Don't compare your partner to anyone else.

5. **Keep your questions down**
Don't ask questions about really personal stuff that relates to someone of the opposite sex. You can do without bonding in soul with anyone except your partner, your family and close friends of the same sex.

6. **Keep your company safe**
Don't be found alone in the private company of someone you're attracted to or even someone you think you could be attracted to.

7. **Keep your hands off**
If you are giving a hug to say goodbye, make sure that it's short and sweet and you only do it in the company of others.

8. **Keep your eyes from wandering**
People who like each other often share glances across a room. Make sure that you're not looking for anyone's eyes across the other side of a room. Only have eyes for the right person.

9. **Keep lines of openness**
If you do find a special attraction that cannot be stopped by points 1–8 above, tell someone and get them to pray for you and work with you in support and wisdom.

10. **Keep your head on**
Don't exchange your birthright for a fleeting pleasure. Weigh up the consequences of sin. Don't get intoxicated by circumstances or by wine. Always be sober and alert.[15]

Can a man stay pure,
Can a heart stay clean,
Can a wife stay faithful,
Or is it just a dream?

Lord I love Your word
I keep it in my heart
That I might not sin
But bless You Lord.
May You take delight
In this heart of mine
Lord I love Your ways
They give me life.

All your ways are good for me Father,
Keep me on Your paths,
Save me from the worthless treasures,
Let me know what lasts.

Chapter 9

Concerning Spiritual Gifts

During the early days of the charismatic movement in Britain there became an increased awareness that gifts of the Spirit remained available to the church. This quickly led to many small and passionate groups of believers exploring 1 Corinthians chapter 12 together. Churches sought to give space for the release of gifts and there followed the inevitable mixture of the good, the bad, and on occasion, the ugly. There was certainly a grassroots movement which had a new desire for prayer and participation. Those outside of the charismatic movement tended to focus on the gift of speaking in tongues, pointing to the potential divisions this newfound fervour may bring. Time has moved on and in the main the church has been invigorated. In fact, the British scene has been remarkably reshaped in terms of worship and openness to spiritual gifts. However, I believe the church would do well to revisit this important subject and ask God for fresh illumination. Some churches have all but abandoned spiritual gifts and others live with the tension of not knowing how best to give opportunity for their release in growing situations.

'I do not want you to be ignorant'

After some years, many still have a feeling that we remain ignorant with regard to the dynamic gifts that are outlined in Corinthians. Often gifts have operated within the context of church meetings only and there have been growing levels of dissatisfaction with our present knowledge. It is my belief that there is much for us to discover and that the world beyond our churches needs to be more fully impacted by their power.

The God who loves to give

God is a giving God. He gives to the church a whole variety of gifts. These gifts come from one God, but are expressed in great diversity. Three passages in the New Testament present us with three lists of gifts. They emphasize in simple terms that God the Father, God the Son, and God the Holy Spirit all give gifts. The three passages are Romans 12, Ephesians 4 and 1 Corinthians 12.

▶ *Gifts of God the Father* (Romans 12)
- Prophecy
- Serving
- Teaching
- Encouraging
- Giving
- Leadership
- Showing mercy

Followed by Romans 12:9 (*love*)

▶ *Gifts of God the Son* (Ephesians 4)
- Apostle
- Prophet
- Evangelist
- Pastors and teachers

Followed by Ephesians 5:1–2 (*love*)

▶ *Gifts of God the Holy Spirit* (1 Corinthians 12)
- Word of wisdom
- Word of knowledge
- Faith
- Gifts of healing
- Miracles
- Prophecy
- Distinguishing between spirits

- Speaking in tongues
- Interpretation of tongues

Followed by 1 Corinthians 13 (*love*)

From this simple outline it is easy to see that the gifts that God gives are in the context of 'body life'. The gifts are not designed to elevate a person, they are to be operated from within the covering of church life. It is also noticeable that each list of gifts is closely followed by a passage on love. The best environment for the use of gifts is the *love* of God. Space does not permit for a close look at each of the gifts, but there are a number of good books available exploring this subject in more detail. I recommend *Hands of Jesus* by Philip Mohabir which is particularly good at framing the gifts in a dynamic mission setting. He writes, 'The ministry gifts are not designed for personal performance or gain. They function best when they operate out of committed relationship as a team. These precious love gifts come from the King Himself to the body, for the body and in the body.'[16]

The nine gifts of the Spirit that are mentioned in 1 Corinthians 12 are like power tools to enable the church to move forward. They are the activity and manifestation of the Holy Spirit and operate by God's grace. The nine gifts can be categorised into three groups:

▶ *Revelation gifts*
- Word of wisdom
- Word of knowledge
- Distinguishing between spirits

▶ *Power gifts*
- Faith
- Gifts of healing
- Miracles

▶ *Vocal gifts*
- Prophecy
- Tongues
- Interpretation of tongues

Empowerment

The letters of Paul to the Corinthians are not only important today because of the problems they address, but also because of the power they promise. There has perhaps never been a time in Britain when the power of the gospel needs demonstrating so much. The post-modern world gives an ideal opportunity for believers who are willing to step out in the power of the Holy Spirit. The supernatural insights made possible by the revelatory gifts of the Holy Spirit can break through into today's sceptical world. What better time than now for the release of supernatural gifts of healing, or even miracles. With the demise of our Health Service and the growing waiting lists, the stage is set for ordinary believers to be available to pray. Could it be that the last thirty years have provided practice time within our church settings and it is now time for courageous believers to take the message to the market-place? This certainly seems to be where the pressure of the Holy Spirit is being directed. It is a movement from maintenance to mission, from the church to the streets.

Mission focus

At a recent Sunday service in New Life, the challenge was given for us to be more bold in our witness. People came forward for prayer at the close of the meeting and a man called Steve asked the Holy Spirit to give him opportunities for witness in the coming week. The following Sunday he gave testimony to the fact that as a result of prayer he had invited his mum to an outreach meeting. Previously she had said, 'No' so he had stopped asking her. Not only did she attend, but also prayed a prayer of commitment at the end. In the same week, Steve overheard that his boss was suffering with a bad back. He later boldly asked her if she would like prayer. To his surprise, she said, 'Yes.' He prayed a simple prayer and later in the week learned that her back had been healed. She confessed that half-an-hour following the prayer the pain had gone. Imagine an army of ordinary people operating in the gifts of the Holy Spirit, working sensitively under our Father's instruction, taking the message of Christ into their places of work and education!

The gift of tongues

A man called Rambabu spoke at Terry Virgo's Conference at Brighton in 2003. I had the honour of speaking in a seminar at the conference and one of the blessings of making the trip to Brighton was being exposed to great teaching and teachers. Rambabu is a great healing evangelist from India who is seeing remarkable things happening in many nations of the world. At the conference he was asked to explain what the secret was to his 'signs and wonders' ministry. He simply answered, 'Speaking in tongues'! For an hour he spoke on the benefits and blessings of speaking in tongues. He saw this gift as a direct phone line to the Father that even the Angel Gabriel was not allowed to answer. He lifted the gift into a high realm of possibilities and testified that before healing crusades he would speak in tongues for six to seven hours at a time. As a result, healings and miracles began to flow. I, like many others, have benefited from the revelations of his ministry and I now often give myself to speaking in tongues when driving on long journeys.

Especially the gift of prophecy

In days when words can so easily bring people down, the church needs to learn how to prophesy. Many live with low levels of self-worth. Destructive words have so often been sown into people over long periods of time: disapproving words, belittling words, demeaning words. Again, this is an ideal time for the church to speak God's words. Many people are passing through life without direction or clarity. Others have no awareness of destiny or future hope. Paul says to the Corinthian church, *'Follow the way of love and eagerly desire spiritual gifts, especially the gift of prophecy'* (1 Corinthians 14:1). Prophetic gifts have rightly been released in the church bringing strength and direction, but I firmly believe that our understanding of prophecy now needs to expand. It is not designed just to strengthen the saints, but is a gift that needs to give teeth to our evangelistic message. In fact, the church not only needs to proclaim a prophetic message, but be a prophetic community of people modelling God's ways to a dying world.

Perhaps I could at this time recommend another life-changing book, *Prophetic Evangelism* by Mark Stibbe.[17] In this book, Mark combines the call to evangelism with the power of the Holy Spirit. He helpfully outlines a number of methods of evangelism endorsed by Scripture. They are:

- Programmed evangelism,
- Presence evangelism,
- Proclamation evangelism,
- Persuasion evangelism,
- Prayer evangelism,
- Power evangelism, and
- Prophetic evangelism.

He goes on to define prophetic evangelism as, 'Simply God using revelatory phenomena to speak to the hearts of those who don't know Jesus.' 1 Corinthians shows how this gift is incredibly important in reaching unbelievers (1 Corinthians 14:24–25).

My task in this chapter has been to whet your appetite to the possibilities of the gifts of the Holy Spirit bringing new dimensions to our witness and evangelism. For some years now, the gifts of the Holy Spirit have been locked into church meetings with some being disappointed that they were not given much space to operate in the gifts. It seems to me that there is plenty of space and untold opportunities for the church to be able to speak God's words into hearts that don't know Him. Communities also need to be impacted by God's word and capture something of God's heart through God's people.

> Lord, let the worship rise from us,
> Like incense from the heart.
> Join with the heavenly songs above,
> Singing hallelujah.
>
> All of creation sings Your praise,
> Age after age, song after song.
> Casting our crowns before Your throne,
> Singing, 'Worthy is the Lamb.'

Light of the world, eternal sun,
From Your face we see glory shining.
The Holy One, the Lamb of God,
With one voice we cry
'You are Worthy.'

Chapter 10

Order!

It was clear that certain things in the Corinthian church were out of order. The questions asked of Paul by the leadership show that they were looking for solutions. The issues facing them were very difficult and required incredible levels of wisdom. What advice were they to give to the congregation? For instance, on the issue of buying cheaper meat from the local market if it had been dedicated to idols? On one hand there were economic restraints and on the other issues of conscience. How would they define weak Christians, or strong Christians? Should they set rules and regulations in place? After all, this was a new church and there weren't too many blueprints around. This is why Paul's letters were so important. He commended them for the progress they were making, but also spoke into areas of disorder. Though many of these must be seen in the context of the culture of the day, there are clear principles given by Paul that can help us today. In fact, twenty-first century church leaders face incredibly difficult situations. Increasingly, all sorts of teaching, some clearly tainted by other religions or humanistic values, have bombarded people attending churches. Pastors who say, 'The Bible says . . . ' run the risk of hearing the words, 'But that was then, we live in a different world now!' This is clearly a day to ask God for wisdom and courage.

It is certainly true that Paul spoke into issues that were of particular importance in Corinth. The whole issue of veils, head coverings, or length of hair, seems outside our frame of reference. However, the principles that Paul addresses are highly relevant today. The root issue of the head-covering situation in Corinth was to do with *order*. Warren Wiersbe writes, 'Eastern society at that time was very jealous over its women. Except for the Temple prostitutes, the women wore long hair and, in public, wore a covering over their heads ... Paul sought to restore order by reminding the Corinthians that God had made a difference between men and women, that each had a proper place in God's economy. There were also appropriate customs that symbolised these relationships and reminded both men and women of their correct places in the divine scheme.'[18] Sadly, in church history certain of Paul's directives have been used to suggest that women are inferior to men. In fact the Christian faith brought freedom and hope particularly to women, children and slaves. The local church was most likely the only fellowship in the Roman Empire that gave dignity to all people regardless of background, gender or social standing. So, in the clutter of today's world, what principles need to be established or re-established among God's people?

Home life

As soon as we talk about 'family' in today's world we need to walk with sensitivity. We cannot now easily define what we mean by 'family'. In a day of rising divorce levels and the increasing reticence of people to enter into binding commitments, the Bible has much to say. It is clear that in the Scriptures the home is the building block for the church. Paul, writing to Timothy and Titus, makes it clear that leaders who are released into churches need to be of good standing in the home and in society. Increasingly, there is an opportunity for Christians to model an alternative lifestyle. This has to do with receiving Jesus as Lord over the home. It will require keeping the home 'clean' and seeing the love of Christ released into the family. God's order should be welcomed, not in terms of restraint, but release.

1 Corinthians 11 is well worth a read in *The Message: The Bible in Contemporary Language* as it gives freshness to this passage. Here's a taster:

> *'In a marriage relationship there is authority from Christ to husband and from husband to wife. The authority of Christ is the authority of God. Any man, who speaks with God, or about*

> *God, in a way that shows a lack of respect for the authority of*
> *Christ, dishonours Christ. In the same way, a wife who speaks*
> *with God in a way that shows a lack of respect for the authority*
> *of her husband dishonours her husband. Worse, she dis-*
> *honours herself – an ugly sight, like a woman with her head*
> *shaved.'*   (1 Corinthians 11:3–6, *The Message*[19])

Nowhere is Paul arguing that women are subservient to men.
There is a need for love and mutual support within families
and for the establishment of God's order, rather than man's
pecking order. Again, in the words of *The Message*, '*And since*
virtually everything comes from God anyway, let's quit going
through these "who's first" routines' (1 Corinthians 11:12).

Church life

There also needs to be order within church life. There are a
number of safeguards in the Scriptures that cover the whole
realm of authority and submission – guidelines that govern
how leaders should behave towards members of the fellowship, and how those members should behave towards their
leaders. In the New Testament a plurality of leadership is
always recommended. By character, leaders should not be self-
seeking or dominant; they are there to serve God's people in
humility. There should be order among the various ministries
of the church and those who are called to rule, and all must be
submitted to the overall leadership of Jesus who is established
as the head of the church.

The Corinthian church had become unbalanced in a
number of areas. One of the biggest problems was disorder in
their public meetings. There was confusion about the proper
operation of spiritual gifts and much disorder around the
Lord's Supper.

The party spirit, already addressed by Paul, was working
strongly in the love feasts. These were *agape* meals where
people ate together, then most likely concluded with the
breaking of bread, remembering the death and resurrection
of Christ. Social groupings had developed within these feasts.
The rich people often bought food for themselves, while
poorer members of the church went hungry. Yes, these were
feasts where the love of Christ should be shared! Some

members were even getting drunk in these gatherings and heightened emotions gave way to a twisting of something that was designed to be a blessing to the whole church.

Paul also brought teaching on the proper use of spiritual gifts. It again seems that some may have developed an elitist mindset and took pride in displaying their many gifts before the congregation. Paul made it clear that there was a time to speak and a time to be silent. The use of gifts was not an opportunity for personal ambition. Prophetic words needed to be subject to careful 'weighing' to test their authenticity. It was not appropriate to shout out at certain times in the service, *'For God is not a God of disorder but of peace'* (1 Corinthians 14:33). Paul goes on to write, *'Everything should be done in a fitting an orderly way'* (verse 40). Of course, the order of God and the order of man can be quite different. Man's order unfortunately has tended to straightjacket the church. However, Corinthians teaches us that leaders need to lead. Ultimately, under the authority of God, leaders must not shirk responsibility.

Crossing lines

So who in each church sets the boundary lines for the use of spiritual gifts and where should they be drawn? In thirty years of ministry, this has been a question constantly asked in leadership gatherings. Some of us have suffered at the hands of well-meaning, but heavy-handed leaders who prescribed how the Christian life should be lived. Sadly, some of these leaders proved to be less godly off the platform than on it. Years of experience have taught me that sometimes when leaders are very hard on certain issues, these are actually the weaknesses they are grappling with. I remember once sitting in a friend's room in America listening to a TV preacher hammering sexual sins, only to hear a few months later of his fall into immorality. I have had times when people have questioned me about whether, as a Christian leader, I should own a TV. One friend strongly challenged me on this issue. He left everything and joined a commune where only the elders were permitted to read daily newspapers. Today, he no longer holds to the Christian faith at all.

The greatest danger today is that we let everyone decide for themselves. Ultimately, all must choose their way in life, but there are lines that are drawn in Scripture. Perhaps the following suggestions of 'how to say the difficult things' will be of practical use to leaders needing to challenge members of their fellowship.

Don't say:	Say:
You should not have a television	You should be careful what you watch
You should never drink wine	You should never get drunk
You should not go to the cinema or theatre	You should be careful what you watch
You should not listen to secular music	You should be selective in what you listen to
You should not marry a particular person	You should be obedient to what the Scriptures say

Leaders should be interested in every member of the church, bringing guidance and godly counsel. All of us should speak out if we see things that are out of balance or if we perceive that boundary lines are being moved. We all need God's order in our lives.

Chapter 11

Around the Lord's Table

I well remember family meals around the table when, as a boy, dinner was served at 12 noon. I can also remember my dad's prodding finger in the small of my back and the words, 'Don't slouch at the table.' On occasions, the length of my hair along with my manners were also discussed in detail. Mum would usually speak in my defence as a peacemaker, trying to ensure that family times together were guarded. Today, these kinds of family meals are often under threat. The busyness of people's lives, together with the invasion of the television, have relegated family times to special occasions. This has given less opportunity for quality times of sharing. Being around the table is the time when the family is together enjoying one another's company.

Table time in the Corinthian church had become difficult. Some simply did not want to sit together and the tablecloth had been stained through bad behaviour and division. Paul, as a priority, passes something on to them that he has directly received from the Lord (1 Corinthians 11:25). He spoke to them of the importance of bread and wine – signs of Christ's sacrificial love. Times of communion were to be times of thanksgiving; they were to be times of remembering the Lord. The Corinthians had dishonoured the table and, as a result of carelessness, God had disciplined them. *'That is why many among you are weak and sick, and a number of you have fallen asleep'* (1 Corinthians 11:30). The communion is meant to be a place of fellowship and spiritual growth.

This issue also stands as a challenge to today's church. How often is communion an afterthought or some kind of appendage at the end of the meeting for the keen believers? In certain quarters of the church, this meal has been relegated to an occasional observance. The content of our communion also needs careful consideration. It should not become merely a ritual where words are read routinely and where there is no sense of genuine friendship and fellowship – a religious exercise devoid of reality. There is no doubt that in the early church, communion was in the context of a full meal and people often broke bread in their home. Its context was an environment of joy with an awareness of the favour of God (Acts 2:46–47). It is my belief that today's church would do well to revisit this new covenant meal and ensure its life is preserved and its importance recognised. With that in mind, I offer the following four methods that address the varying facets of the communion meal:

► *Looking back*

Firstly, there is an opportunity to look back. It is always good to remember. Communion allows us to think back to the night Jesus was betrayed, when He took bread and broke it. We must never forget that His body was broken for us and His blood was shed. This is more than just a nostalgic glance at a past family occasion, but a genuine opportunity to remember Christ's death with thanksgiving.

► *Looking ahead*

Before we were married, there were times when Irene and I would sit together and try to imagine what the future would bring. We wondered how many children we would have and what they would look like. Would they inherit granddad's ears, or grandma's moles? What kind of house would we live in and what would the future hold for us? The beauty of the Lord's Table is that though the future will have its challenges, it will only be *'until he comes'* (1 Corinthians 11:26). Looking to the return of Christ brings great hope and motivation to the church.

► *Looking inward*

Paul writes, *'A man ought to examine himself before he eats of the bread and drinks of the cup'* (1 Corinthians 11:28). The Corinthians were very good at examining others, but not so good at examining themselves. I guess that we often fall into the same trap. I still find myself listening to sermons hoping that a certain person is taking note, as this could be a life-changing experience for them. As a preacher, it is so easy to get a sermon for others, but fail to apply it to oneself. All of us need to regularly examine our own hearts.

▶ *Looking around*

This is perhaps the hardest dimension of the Lord's Supper. It is not just a personal meeting with the Lord, but a corporate meeting with His people. The people on the opposite side of the table really matter. The Lord's Supper is a meal for the whole family. If we love God we must also love His family. If things are wrong between ourselves and others, this is the time to put them right. However, it is not the place to unload all our problems onto a poor unsuspecting brother or sister who, before we came to ask forgiveness of them, had believed that we had always loved and honoured them! I remember one communion service when a lady publicly told Irene that she had never ever liked her and asked for her forgiveness. Irene duly offered her forgiveness, but always remained puzzled as to what it was that had caused this person to dislike her. Sometimes we can unburden our own souls and leave the meeting feeling free, but have placed our burdens onto another's shoulders. Maybe they had come to church feeling happy, but leave feeling sad and rejected.

I believe we need to give regular opportunities for the Lord's Supper. It was here that some of the most intimate moments were shared between Jesus and His disciples. It was the place where motives were questioned and where commitments were made. It was the place for real heart-searching and where the words, *'Surely not I'* (Mark 14:19) seemed appropriate. It was ultimately the place of betrayal. It has always amazed me that people so often bite the hand that feeds them. Communion is a place of close encounter with God and with one another. Strangely, it was at the table where the disciples discussed among themselves which of them would betray the Master. The potential to do so was within all of them and remains in all of us. They also disputed together, which of them was considered to be the greatest (Luke 22:24). Each time the Lord's Supper is celebrated, we declare that He is the greatest and we are His servants. Communion is a time of thanksgiving and joyful anticipation because our future is secure in Him. The following thoughts, though simple, remain a challenge to us all:

▶ *More hugs*
I believe we need to work at the sense of friendship and fellowship which we as believers enjoy together. I'm not suggesting that we need to go back into our history and sing, 'Bind us together' looking into each other's eyes. However, I also hope we do not slip back into the kind of formality where we hardly acknowledge one another's existence. Communion should be a time of vibrant fellowship where the love and peace of Christ is shared.

▶ *More time*
I have already mentioned that in some circles, communion appears to be an afterthought. Our programmes are busy and our time is so limited. I hope that we will begin to think of communion more in terms of the dignity of a relaxed evening dinner, than the dash for a quick bite before rushing back into activity. We need time to consider the Lord and to appreciate one another.

▶ *More thought*
Perhaps it is time to creatively revisit communion. We do not need to 'ring the changes' just for the sake of it, but though the substance of the truth we celebrate remains the same, there is plenty of space for discovering new and exciting ways of approaching the table.

> When I'm feeling tired,
> When my love grows cold,
> Is when I call to you,
> You are never far.
>
> When you hear my song
> Coming from the heart,
> Is when you hold me close,
> I am lost in you.

Once I've tasted of your wine
Nothing else is the same,
I am faint with love.
You are everything to me,
How can I find a way
For my heart to love you more?

When the winds of change
Bring me to my knees.
You're the strength I find,
In your open arms.

Once I've tasted of your wine
Nothing else is the same,
I am faint with love.
You are everything to me,
How can I find a way
For my heart to love you more?

(Paul Simpson-Parry. Copyright © 1998)

Chapter 12

Suffering

Another challenge to the charismatic church is the issue of suffering. It has been important for the church to re-emphasise healing and to restore a positive attitude towards people enjoying the abundant life God promises, however, there has been little space for a theology of suffering, but rather a tendency to equate suffering, sickness and pain too readily with some sin or inadequacy in the person involved. In a fallen world the truth is that all humanity will face suffering at some time.

I remember a friend of mine reviewing his theology when, in his thirties, he was hit severely by the childhood ailment of chickenpox, a disease he confessed he could not get. Even the inclusion of this piece of information can very quickly cause 'lines to be drawn'. Some would take the view that no Christian should ever be sick, while others see sickness as some kind of virtue given by God to produce character. I personally do not stand with either of these extremes. I believe that God wants us to walk in wholeness, but the fullness of the kingdom has not yet found its ultimate release in this dark world. We are not immune to the effects that sin has unleashed. Philip Yancey writes, 'A sick person is not un-spiritual. Christian faith does not magically equip us with a germ-free, hermetically-sealed space suit to protect against the dangers of earth. That would insulate us from complete identification with the world – a luxury God did not allow his Son.'[20]

Paul's letters to the Corinthians open up all kinds of issues with regard to suffering. Much of this is laced with Paul's own personal story and offers hope to all who suffer. Often when Paul writes on this subject, he uses strong contrasts which highlight the mystery of God's dealings with us. The last thing that sufferers need is trite answers or condemning words. People who have it all worked out with prescriptive formulas for health and success worry me. Sometimes Paul's description of his life is a far cry from today's success manuals. Perhaps for a few moments we can lay down our preconceived ideas and look at the Scriptures. My perceptions or interpretations of these letters may not fully line up with yours, but I believe we need to keep revisiting these important truths.

'Apart from the Lord of glory, whose sufferings completely eclipse the pains of any of his servants, Paul appears as one of the great sufferers of Christian history.' So writes Herbert Carson.[21] Paul's sufferings were numerous and varied, affecting him physically, emotionally and spiritually. However, it is noticeable that in his communication, Paul never majors on the negatives. He recognises the contrasts that come our way in the cycle of life.

Sweet and sour

In 2 Corinthians 6, Paul intermingles the good with the bad. He has learned a level of contentment and trust that enables him to focus on his goals however circumstances turn out. His testimony is realistic – he doesn't just share the good stories. The two columns below give a visual record of his journey.

Great endurance	Purity
Troubles	Understanding
Hardships	Patience
Distresses (verse 4)	Kindnesses
Beatings	In the Holy Spirit
Imprisonments	Sincere love (verse 6)
Riots	Truthful speech
Hard work	Power of God
Sleepless nights	Weapons of righteousness (verse 7)
Hunger (verse 5)	Glory (verse 8)
Dishonour (verse 8)	Good report
Bad report	Genuine (verse 8)

Regarded as impostors (verse 8)	Known
Unknown	Living
Dying	Not killed (verse 9)
Sorrowful	Rejoicing
Poor	Making many rich
Having nothing	Possessing everything (verse 10)

The left-hand column could perhaps be seen as Paul's 'Monday morning' testimony. On reading both columns, it would be hard to imagine that each set of circumstances and commendations belong to the same person – but they do. So it is with us. Though the contrast is hardly likely to be as stark, the truth is our lives consist of sun and rain, good and bad. Paul writes in this kind of way to emphasise the fact that both columns are linked. The incredible contrast in verse ten quotes, *'Having nothing, yet possessing everything'* which paints a grace picture that makes little sense outside kingdom thinking. Yet for Paul both statements are true. The hardship is producing something. Patience, for example, is more likely to develop in us if things are withheld. The darkness of the sorrowful day makes the day of rejoicing even more colourful. Great endurance creates new levels of understanding in us, and our own poverty causes joy to well up within us at the privilege of making many rich.

2 Corinthians 11 opens the issue up even more fully when Paul *boasts* about his suffering, because he knows that through his weakness the strength of God will be seen more readily. In this chapter every kind of suffering is mentioned.

Physical suffering

Paul had frequently experienced life in prison and knew what it was to be wrongly accused and misunderstood. He had been severely flogged and exposed to death again and again. On five occasions he had received thirty-nine lashes; three times had been beaten by rods, and on one occasion had been stoned. I cannot imagine many of today's ministry people not griping over how unfair life had become. I, for one, would have made sure that everybody knew what a sacrifice I was making for the gospel!

Psychological suffering

Often Paul had faced uncertainty, pressure, danger and deprivation. He writes about constantly being on the move. This lifestyle meant he would not know where he would stay or what he would eat. Anyone in ministry who has travelled for very long knows that the novelty soon wears off. Paul was not used to travelling 'business class', nor could he lay his weary bones down at the Hilton. Incidentally, I would not have had a problem if he had enjoyed those privileges, and anyway, being able to travel by ship tells me he was no pauper. However, he was shipwrecked on three occasions, which could not have been good for the blood pressure. 2 Corinthians 11:26 is Paul's 'danger' verse: he had known danger from rivers, bandits, Jews and Gentiles; he had known danger in the city, danger in the country, danger at sea and danger from false brothers. Who now would like to be an apostle? Due to his hardworking lifestyle Paul was often deprived of sleep. He had known what it was to be hungry, thirsty, cold and naked. Added to this was the daily pressure and concern for all the churches (verse 28). Though I only possess a small understanding of this, I have felt a strange weight on occasions with regard to churches we serve. I find myself looking for people I have met on previous visits, hoping they are still 'running the race'.

Relational pressure

As we have already examined, Paul was often misunderstood. The Corinthian church had questioned his commitment on a number of occasions. We will see later the number of broken relationships that he had to survive. He was also compared with so-called 'super apostles' who were apparently more charismatic and outwardly gifted (2 Corinthians 11:5). The frustration for Paul was that he knew instinctively that these men were in the ministry for their own gain and had hoodwinked the believers. He writes, *'For such men are false apostles, deceitful workmen, masquerading as apostles of Christ'* (verse 13). Perhaps 2 Corinthians 6:11–13 best sums up some of the frustration he feels. In these verses Paul, with some measure of vulnerability, declares to the Corinthians how openly he had sought to share his heart with them. He writes,

'*We are not withholding our affection from you, but you are withholding yours from us*' (verse 12). How hard it is when we share deeply with people only to be faced with no response. I can think of a number of occasions where I have opened up vulnerable areas of my life, expecting that others would also share their struggles. When there is no feedback we can then quickly regret sharing and the tendency is to withdraw. This affects our trust of others and we're unlikely to share as deeply a second time. Recognising this Paul writes, '*As a fair exchange – I speak as to my children – open wide your hearts also*' (verse 13). For relationships to mature we need to encourage two-way communication. Some people create a potential power-base by knowing our weaknesses, but keeping their own hearts closed. The inference is that we are the ones with the problem. They may emphasise this further by offering to pray for us.

Sickness

I have not so far included this area in Paul's suffering, as it is a subject of debate and difference of opinion. Some would see Paul's '*thorn in the flesh*' (2 Corinthians 12:7) as some kind of physical disorder, possibly to do with an eye condition. I personally think this was more likely to do with the constant attack of the Judaizers who relentlessly worked against Paul's gospel of grace. One thing is certain, however. Whatever this was, a '*messenger of Satan*' tormented him. This was an enemy work that would not go away. We also know that there were occasions when members of Paul's team were ill, some seriously, and that Timothy had stomach problems that needed attention from time to time.

Apostle in a basket

In all the suffering that Paul endured, the picture of this great ministry gift of Christ to the church being lowered from a window in the wall of Damascus captures a moment of indignity. Paul's future was seen to be hanging in God's providential hand. He writes, '*If I must boast, I will boast of the things that show my weakness*' (2 Corinthians 11:30). He had learned that in the weakest moment God's strength breaks through.

Advice for emerging pastors

Some time ago I embarked on a study of the pastoral epistles. To my surprise, I became aware of a 'struggle' element I had not noticed as strongly before. I particularly noticed the hardship Paul had faced in his pastoral ministry and the serious issues that had crept into the life of the church. I began reading of people who had *'shipwrecked their faith'* (1 Timothy 1:19), of false doctrines and heresies that needed withstanding (1 Timothy 1:3), of people who had wandered away (1 Timothy 1:6) and of others who had abandoned their faith (1 Timothy 4:1). I read of false teaching that had spread like gangrene (2 Timothy 2:17) and also godlessness in the last days (2 Timothy 3:1–5). It became clear that Paul was warning Timothy and Titus, two emerging pastors, to be prepared to *'fight the good fight'* (1 Timothy 1:18). Life would not be easy. They would need to be strong.

My eyes were also open to some of the pain that Paul was facing. These books give special insight into the rejection and hurt that are part of the package which comes with the high calling of ministry. In this section, I have chosen to major on the relational suffering Paul had to work through as I believe this remains one of the hardest areas of Christian ministry.

Those who desert

I have decided to mainly examine 2 Timothy chapter 4 verses 9–22. In my Bible the heading is, 'Personal remarks'. It is as though we catch a glimpse of a page of Paul's diary, which reveals something of his personal pain. *'For Demas, because he loved this world, has deserted me and gone to Thessalonica.'* How painful this must have been. Demas had shown all the qualities necessary for future church leadership, but there were stronger and more ambitious forces working in his life. He was unlikely to reach his God-ordained destiny. Later Paul says, *'At my first defence, no-one came to my support, but everyone deserted me'* (verse 16). On my low days this verse is an encouragement. I would have thought people would have flocked to his defence. There may well be some red-faced people in glory who are kicking themselves for not making themselves available to defend Paul's honour. They did not know then how famous he would be one day (I jest of course, as there will be no red-faced people in heaven!). In 2 Timothy 1:15 there is an even more shocking piece of information. *'You know that everyone in the province of Asia has deserted me, including Phygelus and Hermogenes.'* I can imagine a couple of people leaving. But the whole of Asia? There must have been times when Paul felt a failure.

Those who move on

Inevitably, those who once fellowshipped alongside us, move on and go elsewhere. Though this is not always negative it can, nonetheless, often be painful. Crescans has now moved to Galatia, Titus to Dalmatia and Tychicus (quite a small man) to Ephesus. Reading between the lines, Paul is really feeling it as he writes, *'Only Luke is with me'* (2 Timothy 4:11). Those in ministry thrive on relationship and it is painful when people leave. I know that in my own circles I am perceived as being too possessive and wanting things to remain as they have always been. I know there is truth in this, but it still saddens me when people who have walked alongside me for some time look for new challenges elsewhere.

Those who cause harm

There are, of course, more destructive breakdowns of relation-ship. Paul is not afraid to name people who have caused discredit to the ministry. I guess today we would be more nervous at being quite as forthright. Paul writes, *'Alexander the metalworker did me a great deal of harm. The Lord will repay him for what he has done'* (verse 14). Most ministries have their 'Alexanders' who cause incredible heartache. Sadly, there are Alexanders out there who feel they are the ones who are hard done by. I can only imagine what Alexander was spreading about Paul and unfortunately people are influenced by these kinds of people.

Those who serve

There are of course many people who remain faithful. The danger is that we can easily take these people for granted.

Paul makes mention of Onesiphorus who we know was a faithful servant. His name means, 'Help bringer'. There are always good people who refresh us rather than drain us. At a leadership meeting a couple of years ago I pronounced his name as, 'One-is-for-us' and recognised that though all of Asia may have left, there is always one who remains.

What is it all about?

Why all the suffering? Why all the pain? Sometimes we revert to classic answers like, 'His thoughts are higher than our thoughts and His ways higher than our ways,' but often such words feel inadequate. Although there is no full answer to this, Paul does bring some revelation in 2 Corinthians 1. Here we see, *'The God of all comfort'*. In some remarkable way, the God of all comfort brings comfort into our lives so that in due time we can bring comfort to others. Our sufferings help us to identify with the sufferings of others, yet not only to identify with them, but also to bring help, support and ministry to them. God has blessed us with these blessings and we can bless others. *'For just as the sufferings of Christ flow over into our lives, so also through Christ our comfort overflows'* (2 Corinthians 1:5). Suffering is producing something in us:

> *'We also rejoice in our sufferings, because we know that suffering produces perseverance; perseverance, character; and character, hope. And hope does not disappoint us, because God has poured out his love into our hearts by the Holy Spirit, whom he has given us.'* (Romans 5:3–5)

Most people who, like Paul, have endured much suffering will tell you that during their darkest hour, God supplied a grace for that event or circumstance which far outstripped the pain of suffering. The all-sufficient One will supply grace for every situation in life that will be *more than* sufficient. I would like to close this chapter with a reminder of some of the verses that speak about this grace. Somehow, though we don't deserve it, God always manages to bring light into the darkest of times. This can give us hope, even in the midst of great trials.

Surprising grace

It has been my experience that grace turns up when we least expect it. We are surprised that in our sufferings, good begins to emerge. This is the turning of that which was intended to harm us, into something that ultimately produces fruitfulness and goodness in us. This grace really is amazing!

> *'And God is able to make all grace abound to you, so that in all things, at all times, having all that you need, you will abound in every good work.'* (2 Corinthians 9:8)

Surpassing grace

> *'And in their prayers for you, their hearts will go out to you, because of the surpassing grace God has given you.'* (2 Corinthians 9:14)

This is grace beyond what we could expect. We get better than the best as far as God is concerned. Paul goes on to say, *'Thanks be to God for his indescribable gift'* (verse 15). When we are tempted to feel sorry for ourselves, we simply need to be reminded of what God has done and to remember the sufferings of our Lord Jesus Christ, which have brought us eternal life.

Sufficient grace

There is always enough grace to bring us through. We may feel, as Paul did, that problems should have been removed because we prayed. But prayer is not making God do what we want; it is the aligning of ourselves with His greater purposes. He really does know what is best for us.

> *'My grace is sufficient for you, for my power is made perfect in weakness.'* (2 Corinthians 12:9)

> I believe in angels,
> God's messengers of fire.
> I believe in prophets,
> Who with God's word inspire.

I believe in miracles
And that the strongholds fall,
And I believe in Jesus
The highest name of all.

I believe in worship
That touches heaven's throne.
I believe His Spirit
Renews the faithful one.
I believe the Word of God,
His truth revealed to all.
Yes, I believe in Jesus,
The highest name of all.

[*Chorus*]
It's the highest name,
The name that's over all.
It's the highest name,
The name on which we call. [*repeat*]

I believe that suff'ring
And martyrs' cries will cease.
I believe that healing
Will find its full release.
And I believe the Son of God
Word of Heaven come.
Trust in His salvation
Born of faith alone.

I believe revival
Will touch the earth again.
I believe His kingdom
Will rule without an end.
I believe that unity
Will see His blessing fall.
For I believe in Jesus
The highest name of all.

(Stuart Bell, Johnny Markin & Paul Cruickshank.
Copyright © 1998,
Sovereign Lifestyle Music)

Don't Lose Heart

Lose a job and a new one may well emerge.
Lose a friend and you will find another.
Lose your vision and glasses may help.
Lose your perspective and through friendship and
         counsel, direction returns.
Lose your hair and you can wear a hat.
Lose a parent and years later healing comes.
Lose your strength and rest can revitalise.
Lose something precious and the insurance will
         eventually pay up!
Lose your power and prayer can change things.
Lose your fire and a word from God can rekindle it.
But if you lose heart, you lose everything.

*'Therefore, since through God's mercy we have this ministry,
we do not lose heart.'*   (2 Corinthians 4:1)

*'Therefore we do not lose heart. Though outwardly we are
wasting away, yet inwardly we are being renewed day by day.'*
                                        (2 Corinthians 4:16)

Chapter 13

Overflowing Generosity

Charismatic churches ought to be generous churches. There are two key passages in Paul's letters to the Corinthians – 1 Corinthians 16 and 2 Corinthians 8 – where Paul advises the believers on the subject of giving. Whenever Paul begins to address an important new topic in his letters, he typically starts with the words 'Now about . . . ', e.g. marriage (1 Corinthians 7:1); food sacrificed to idols (1 Corinthians 8:1), and spiritual gifts (1 Corinthians 12:1). It seems to me that Paul attached the same importance to each of these topics, yet historically charismatics have given much more of their time and attention to 'Now about spiritual gifts . . . ' and perhaps should give more time to 'Now about the collection . . . ' (1 Corinthians 16:1). For too long churches have viewed collections or offerings as necessary but embarrassing. Giving is often viewed as something that comes after the worship, instead of being a part of our worship.

Firstly, let's examine 1 Corinthians chapter 16. Paul is not talking here about tithing, but about taking a collection for a group of God's people in Jerusalem who were in need. However, there are principles here that cover all aspects of giving which are foundational for all churches at all times.

Systematic giving

The Corinthians were encouraged by Paul to *'set aside'* a sum of money each week (1 Corinthians 16:2). This was a commitment rather than a random gift. It would have been relatively easy to give a 'one-off' gift, but this required both planning and discipline.

Sensible giving

Paul advises that each person should set aside a gift that is *'in keeping with his income'* (verse 2). The Scriptures are very practical here. Giving should always be in faith, but we should not give what we do not have. This is where leadership needs to be particularly careful. It is so easy to manipulate people from platforms. It is appropriate to stimulate faith through God's word, but it is irresponsible to pressurise or heap condemnation onto the congregation. Jesus is more interested in the heart and attitude of the giver than the amount of money given. It is true, I believe, that Jesus still watches what we give. He notices if we pretend to drop something in the bag as it passes by. In Luke 21 there is the account of Jesus seeing both what the rich put into the Temple treasury and also what a poor widow gave. He went on to commend the widow by saying, *'This poor widow has put in more than all the others'* (Luke 21:3). Her copper coins represented incredible sacrifice. She actually put in all that she had. The Temple could not operate on what she gave, but it could if everyone gave as she gave.

Saving for giving

Next Paul writes about *'Saving . . . up'* (verse 2) to give gifts. Here is the principle of accumulation. It is amazing how much we can give by this method. Often in Britain we begin with the premise that we can't afford to give. In the last few years in our home church in Lincoln, we have set in motion a 'faith pledge' concept for our missions giving, where people plan a regular system of giving each month. During the last year our church gave over £100,000 beyond our normal giving to mission activities. We have a long way to go, but this kind of approach helps to break a poverty mentality. If the Christian message is as important as we say it is, then it will be increasingly important to 'put our money where our mouth is'!

Secure giving

Some churches have been discredited by large sums of money not being adequately accounted for. Paul takes accountability very seriously. *'I will give letters of introduction to the man you approve and send them with your gift to Jerusalem'* (1 Corinthians 16:3). Paul wanted the church to know that everything was being adequately overseen. Today it is important that our works are well governed through the correct channels of oversight both spiritually and practically. It is a great joy to be a part of God's work throughout the world. Investing in the Kingdom of God brings such good returns.

The second passage worth looking at is 2 Corinthians chapter 8, which in my Bible is headed 'Generosity Encouraged'. This passage begins with the words, *'And now, brothers, we want you to know about the grace that God has given ...'* (2 Corinthians 8:1). Generosity is not just a human response, but is based upon the grace of God. Just as spiritual gifts are dependent upon grace, so is giving. We can only give due to His generosity extended towards us. In this chapter Paul points the Corinthians to the example of the Macedonian churches. Churches in Philippi, Thessalonica and Berea were modelling an unusual level of generosity that could only be attributed to God's grace.

An example not a hard-sell plea

Paul uses these churches as a living example of people who are not naturally able to give much. Yet, God's people in Macedonia were experiencing God's favour, which caused them to resource God's work far beyond what they could have imagined was possible. Look at the contrasts Paul outlines:

Severe trial	Overflowing joy (verse 2)
Extreme poverty	Rich generosity (verse 2)
As they were able	Beyond their ability (verse 3)

Some of the most generous of God's people are found to be those who naturally don't have much. It is not usually the rich who provide the bulk of a churches finances. It is mostly the ordinary people who are supernaturally supplied. This supply becomes an expression of God's grace and things then get resourced and needs met. When grace is in great supply, giving is not a duty but a pleasure. The believers that Paul is referring to had *'urgently pleaded with* [Paul] *for the privilege of sharing in this service to the saints'* (2 Corinthians 8:4). It is so refreshing when this kind of grace flows. This grace causes people to move from duty to genuine and joyful Christian service.

Not a command but a comparison

Paul is careful to say, *'I am not commanding you, but I want to test the sincerity of your love by comparing it with the earnestness of others'* (2 Corinthians 8:8). It is always good to be challenged by those who are further on in this realm than we are. I have greatly benefited from seeing large resources released through ordinary people. Incidentally, generosity can become a life-style. How generous are we in our everyday lives? For instance, if we go out for a meal with friends do we fumble around to find our wallet, thus giving others time to pay, or do we suggest going 'Dutch' (whatever that means!) would be a good idea; or are we pleased to take the bill and with a smile say, 'My pleasure'? The Corinthian church excelled in many things, but Paul's challenge was, *'See that you also excel in this grace of giving'* (verse 7).

Of course, Paul knew that the ultimate challenge to this kind of lifestyle was not primarily a generous Christian, but Jesus Himself. Jesus is always the one who stands above all as an example. Paul says, *'For you know the grace of our Lord Jesus Christ, that though he was rich, yet for your sakes he became poor, so that you through his poverty might become rich'* (verse 9). Willingness of the heart is the thing that really matters, and then of course we need to follow through in practical application (verse 12). Just as God's grace was released through the provision of manna in the wilderness, so God promises to meet all our needs. *'As it is written, "He who gathered much did not have too much, and he who gathered little did not have too little"'* (verse 15). Like all things in church life, the best results are achieved when all God's people take responsibility together.

Not haphazard, but ordered and accountable

Paul makes it clear that overseeing finances is a very serious responsibility. This accountability was expressed in sending

Titus to oversee things. There is reference given to the fact that a person had been designated by the church itself to accompany the distribution of the offering (verse 19). It is worth noting here that administering grace is also vitally important. Paul says, *'We want to avoid any criticism of the way we administer this liberal gift. For we are taking pains to do what is right, not only right in the eyes of the Lord but also in the eyes of men'* (verses 20–21). I am deeply grateful to God for administrators who help us with increasingly complex systems and thankfully, larger offerings. In the past the church has often been heard to say, 'Well, we're only here to please the Lord,' but it also would be good and healthy to please the Charity Commissioners as well! May God's grace flow through generous communities of God's people who are determined to make a difference.

Chapter 14

The Way of Love

Paul describes love as the 'most excellent way' and so love should be at the centre of all that our churches are, and all that they seek to do. Following his discourse on spiritual gifts, 1 Corinthians 13 is really the heart of Paul's letter. The content of this chapter stands in incredible contrast to the earthbound issues of division, immorality and dispute that have been addressed earlier. It is as though we are breathing different air in the higher atmosphere of these verses. Throughout time, humanity has sought to find this pathway of love, but has opted to linger on the lower slopes of an imitation of the real thing. Poets have written about love; composers have sung about love; cards are signed with love; couples that are starting out together on a mysterious journey exchange words of love. Love is expressed in smiles and exchanged in acts of kindness. Yet for many it is elusive and for others, unattainable. The Beatles told us that all we needed was love and then they disbanded. For the Christian, love is found in a person – in One who has been given a higher name than any other. He is the One who proclaimed Himself, 'The Way', and His Father is love.

In the Greek language there are different words for love. *Phileo* describes friendship or brotherly love. *Eros* is sexual or physical love; while *agape* is a different kind of love altogether. This is the kind of love that is described as the most excellent way.

There's 'lurve' and there's love

Perhaps the closest we can come to understanding this concept is by examining both 'love' and what the world might appropriately describe as 'lurve' – a word often coined in contemporary film and TV. Lurve, it seems to me, is found on the lower slopes. It often represents genuine desires of human aspiration and heartfelt emotion. At its best, it encapsulates all that is good about man, but at its worst, represents a fallen way that often devalues men and women who were intended for higher things.

Love

The Dictionary of Theology describes *agape* as 'Godlike love that stands in total contrast to all pagan ideas of love in a fallen world ... It is based neither on a felt need in the living person, nor on a desire called forth by some attractive feature in the one loved ... Its source is God and its pattern and inspiration are Jesus Christ.'[22] The word 'love' is very important to Paul. It appears seventy-five times in his letters. He places 1 Corinthians 13 between two sections on charismatic gifts. The issue is not gifts or love, but gifts operating in love. People have wrongly thought that Paul was emphasising that the gifts were not necessary and love was all that was needed. This cannot be the case as he had spent much time endorsing the gifts within a defined church setting. However, what is clear is the warning that gifts without love are ineffective and meaningless. What a challenge to charismatics! Paul's intention is to raise the level of charismatic gifts, working in an atmosphere of love. In Corinth this new kind of love was essential if the church was to be effective. The church was being infected by the culture of Corinth, rather than challenging the prevailing culture of the city in order to bring change. What was needed was the sowing of a different spirit.

The excellent way of love (1 Corinthians 13:1–3)

1 Corinthians 12 closes with a section encouraging the church to desire the greater gifts and then moves directly into the words, *'And now I will show you the most excellent way'* (verse 31). This paves the way for one of the best known chapters in the Bible. I have heard these verses read in countless wedding services and they represent one of the greatest heart-cries of

humanity: the quest for love. The opening verses of this chapter give high prominence to both the gifts of the Spirit and the fruit of the Spirit, particularly categorised by love. F.B. Meyer wrote, 'Faith is the root; hope is the stem; love the perfect flower. You may have faith without hope, and hope without love; but you cannot have love apart from faith and hope.'[23]

Tongues and love

I have often been saddened to notice that speaking in tongues and love do not always seem to go together. Matthew Henry writes, 'It is the charitable heart not the voluble tongue that is acceptable with God.'[24] I am not sure these words capture the whole import of the verse as Paul actually had quite a 'voluble tongue' himself (1 Corinthians 14:18). Nevertheless, without love we are in danger of being *'a resounding gong or a clanging symbol'* (1 Corinthians 13:1). Therefore speaking in tongues is a wonderful and important gift that needs to operate in God's safe environment of love.

Prophecy, knowledge, faith and love

Paul emphasises here that even gifts of the Spirit that operate at a very high level of accuracy or power render us as, *'nothing'* (verse 2) if love is not the motivator. Sadly, we have measured spirituality by the gifts people possess, rather than the calibre of life and the character of the person.

Sacrificial giving, martyrdom and love

Paul says people can actually give everything, even sacrificing their own bodies and yet gain nothing (verse 3) if there is no love cause. The kind of love that is necessary is passionate love for God, unreserved love for people without partiality, and fervent love for the church for which Christ demonstrated His love in the laying down of His life.

The essential character of love (1 Corinthians 13:4–7)

Paul goes on to outline what love is. What follows is really a description of Jesus Himself. This kind of love can change and transform communities and cities.

Love is:	Love is not:
Patient	Envious
Kind	Boastful
Forgiving	Proud
Truthful	Rude
Protecting	Self-seeking
Trusting	Easily angered
Hopeful	
Persevering	

Sadly, in church life we find too many characteristics from the second column. In short, the challenge is to become more like Jesus.

'This is how we know what love is: Jesus Christ laid down his life for us. And we ought to lay down our lives for our brothers.'
(1 John 3:16)

The enduring nature of love (1 Corinthians 13:8–13)

Gifts will cease, they will be stilled and they will pass away. Prophecies, tongues, and words of knowledge remain necessary until perfection comes. They are therefore highly important in today's church, but when Christ returns they will become unnecessary. Until then, we need to encourage the gifts, recognising that they are imperfect because they operate through imperfect people. Love, however, rather than diminishing in importance will be more fully expressed through a purified people. Paul gives pictures of a 'growing-up' or maturing process for the church. A development from a child to a man (verse 11); from a poor reflection to face-to-face meeting (verse 12); and from 'in part' to 'fullness' (verse 12). Our task is to see the bride prepare for the coming King. This leads to a strong link between 'loving' and 'growing'. Faith, hope and love remain, *'But the greatest of these is love'* (verse 13). Love lasts forever because God is love.

Ephesians 4:14–16 show the maturing process necessary for today's church. Rather than being tossed from one idea to another, the church needs to grow up. This maturing process leads into Christ who is the very embodiment of love:

'Instead, speaking the truth in love, we will in all things grow up into him who is the Head, that is, Christ. From him the whole body, joined and held together by every supporting ligament, grows and builds itself up in love, as each part does its work.' (Ephesians 4:15–16)

What Britain needs is a church that is thoroughly charismatic, moving in the gifts of the Holy Spirit and a church that is growing in love. This kind of church will be world-changing.

Oh how I need You God
I've never felt a love so strong
In days of such troubled hearts
You bring freedom and how I long to be
Wholly devoted
Wholly devoted to You.

Oh how I love You Lord
I've never felt like this before
My heart is filled with songs
Of adoration and how I long
To be held
To be held by You.

[*Chorus*]
More and more
I've come to know
Your grace and love for me is so strong.
More and more
I've come to see
How much I need Your power in me
Such overwhelming love.

I can't express this heart of mine
Every day I come to find
That is Your grace You've given to me
So much more
So much more
So much more
More and more.

Chapter 15

Taking Our Stand

There were all kinds of things in Corinth to cause people to give up their faith. Here again we find lessons that have a contemporary relevance for us. The Corinthians believers had to cope with:

- Broken relationships
- Factions
- Law suits

These would keep the best pastoral staff busy. No doubt these kind of things would cause people to say, 'I had enough problems before I joined this church ... I thought Christians would be different ... Even the un-churched would not live that way.' Add to these adverse circumstances, enemy activity, tiredness, deferred hope, unfulfilled promises and you have a seedbed for discontent. In today's cynical world we need to maintain faith and learn how to take our stand.

Sometimes we feel we can only just keep our head above water when pressures come against us. In 1992 Her Majesty Queen Elizabeth II made a speech in which she spoke of the *annus horribilis*. She referred to a horrible year in terms of things that had happened to the Royal family. We all have seasons of trial, but it is what we do and how we react to the trials that are very important. On a personal note, for almost five years we have faced various trials, particularly with sickness in our family, which have made life very difficult. On occasions it has been very tempting to want to 'back-off', but constantly we face the challenge of making sure that, having done all, we continue to stand. Charismatics have often been viewed as people of faith who are relatively 'problem-free'. Some I have known have not been prepared for pressure or hardship and as a result have floundered. My hope is that the following material will help any who are facing severe trials.

What does it mean 'to stand'?

The dictionary defines standing as, 'to have, take or keep a stationary upright position; to remain undisturbed; to endure; resistance to attack or pressure'. Ephesians 6 is a key passage on this subject where the word 'stand' or 'standing' appears four times in the same number of verses. However, I will chiefly confine my material to the letters written to the Corinthians. What does it mean then to stand? Perhaps I could offer the following five suggestions:

▶ *1. Standing is the place of trusting surrender to the will of a loving God.*
How difficult it is to implicitly trust when the pressure is on. A child will gladly jump from a high wall into his father's arms knowing beyond a shadow of a doubt that he will be caught. God may be big, but what kind of a God is He? Can we continue to trust when all hell seems to break out against us? When being chased by bloodthirsty Egyptians, it is not easy to say as Moses did, *'Do not be afraid. Stand firm and you will see the deliverance the* Lord *will bring you today'* (Exodus 14:13). It is one thing to believe on a sunny day that we are safe, but when the clouds gather it can easily be another story. Neither was it easy for King Jehoshaphat to declare, *'You will not have to fight this battle. Take up your positions; stand firm and see the deliverance the* Lord *will give you'* (2 Chronicles 20:17). It is worth noting that on both occasions the children of Israel were told *not* to be afraid, suggesting that fear is a normal response. God wants us to be lifted from the pit and to stand on a firm rock. We must never give up.

It would have been easy for the Corinthian church to look at the actions of God's people and give up. A challenge was equally upon the stronger believers. Paul writes, *'So if you think you are standing firm, be careful that you don't fall!'* (1 Corinthians

10:12). Yes, God could be trusted. The Corinthians needed to know that God was powerfully with them and that if they surrendered He would pull them through, however difficult the circumstance or trial. *'No temptation has seized you except what is common to man. And God is faithful; he will not let you be tempted beyond what you can bear. But when you are tempted, he will also provide a way out so that you can stand up under it'* (1 Corinthians 10:13).

▶ *2. Standing is the place of persistent intercession ushering in the will of God.*

Standing also has to do with standing in the gap on behalf of people and situations. Abraham took this classic position when he stood between Sodom and Gomorrah and a holy God. This meant persistence and even apparent pushiness with the Almighty.

Moses took his stand, supported on the right and left by Aaron and Hur, so that he could extend the rod of God thus enabling Joshua to be victorious in battle.

In a dark world we are called upon to keep our prayer life flowing, so that we may see more breakthroughs. Paul was determined to raise up a standard in Corinth. His constant prayer, coupled with action and resolve, began to lift the church onto higher ground. Prayer needs to be accompanied by the tackling of issues of darkness and injustice. Standing often means holding out for a high standard of righteousness. For the Corinthians, the drift in godless behaviour needed to be stopped. It required people who would stand and be counted; people who were strong and courageous. Paul encouraged them, *'Be on your guard; stand firm in the faith; be men of courage; be strong. Do everything in love'* (1 Corinthians 16:13–14).

▶ *3. Standing is the place of defiant resistance to the desires and designs of the enemy.*

The enemy is against us and we need to stand. Paul says, *'We work with you for your joy, because it is by faith you stand firm'* (2 Corinthians 1:24). We will need faith in God to see that the battle is won. In 2 Corinthians 10 Paul majors on the battle element. He emphasises the fact that the Corinthian believers need to grow in maturity. They had tried to fight battles in carnal ways and expended energy on internal squabbling, not recognising where the true battle was. He writes, *'The weapons we fight with are not the weapons of the world. On the contrary, they have divine power to demolish strongholds. We demolish arguments and every pretension that sets itself up against the knowledge of God, and we take captive every thought to make it obedient to Christ'* (2 Corinthians 10:4–5). We need both divine power and divine weapons.

▶ *4. Standing is the place of strategic positioning for a new move in our lives.*

Joshua was told to stand up after Achan's sin had been discovered. He, like so many of us, was tempted to stay on the floor, but there was more for him to do. Similarly, Jeremiah was told, *'Get yourself ready! Stand up and say to them whatever I command you'* (Jeremiah 1:17).

In 2 Corinthians 1:21–22 Paul writes, *'Now it is God who makes both us and you stand firm in Christ. He anointed us, set his seal of ownership on us, and put his Spirit in our hearts as a deposit, guaranteeing what is to come.'* By the Holy Spirit we are empowered to keep going; to have fresh initiatives and to take new territory. We must not be downcast, we must stand.

▶ *5. Standing is the place of confident praise and worship recognising the rule and reign of God.*

Standing is a suitable position for worship and praise. Nehemiah told the people, *'Stand up and praise the Lord your God, who is from everlasting to everlasting'* (Nehemiah 9:5).

The Levites were to stand every morning to thank and praise the Lord (1 Chronicles 23:30). Peter stood up with the eleven to proclaim God's word to the people (Acts 2:14). The Corinthians needed this attitude. They were not to yield to the prevailing culture of the day. Paul writes, *'But thanks be to God! He gives us the victory through our Lord Jesus Christ. Therefore, my dear brothers, stand firm. Let nothing move you'* (1 Corinthians 15:57–58). As our culture shifts and as standards change we need a people who will stand firm, come what may.

> After I've done everything, I will stand ...
> With my eyes on the King of Kings
> I will stand ... I will stand.

I will stand in confidence
To see the Lord's deliverance
I will stand . . . I will stand.
Of this I'm absolutely sure
I'll see the goodness of the Lord
Yes I will stand.

Because I'm standing with Jesus
I am standing with my King.
Because I'm standing with Jesus
I am standing with my King.

Even in the darkest days, I will stand . . .
And bring a sacrifice of praise . . .
I will stand . . . I will stand.
No matter what is thrown at me
I'll stand against the devil's schemes
I will stand . . . I will stand.
Upright and undisturbed
Unafraid I'm standing firm
Yes, I will stand.
(Stand and I will stand with you . . .)

(Godfrey Birtill.
Copyright © 2003, Thank You Music)

Chapter 16

The Body Principle

Into the fragmentation and factions of the Corinthians church Paul declares, *'Now you are the body of Christ, and each one of you is a part of it'* (1 Corinthians 12:27). Though this may be a familiar concept in today's church, it was pure revelation to the Corinthians. Independence however, has dogged the church through its chequered history and remains a major challenge today. Of course, sometimes we need to break free from any systems or entrapments that bind us, but God's intention is for unity in the church.

In New Testament days, churches were not defined by denomination or belief system, but simply by location. It was 'the church in Corinth' or 'the saints in Ephesus' or 'the Galatian churches'. The issue Paul addresses here is within the 'one church'. Our situation is even more complex today because we so often have disunity *within* churches, and also *between* churches. Many years of church history have created a far from perfect picture.

On 4th July 1776 the USA (then only 13 States) claimed independence from Great Britain. From the American point of view it was important to be freed from the tyranny and despotic rule of George III. There followed 'The Declaration of Independence' when the world was made aware of the new freedom and the American dream was born. Some years ago, I was visiting friends in Pennsylvania on 4th July, enjoying a barbecue and later that evening watching an impressive fireworks display. I remember thinking, 'They're very happy to be rid of us.' Of course, the passage of time changes things and it was only last year, 2003, that I was welcomed by a customs official who said that he was happy I was visiting his country because of the 'special relationship' our two nations enjoyed.

Sometimes it is important for people to have a measure of independence. As children grow older it is important that they move out from under our strong parental control in order to find their own way in life. The ideal is that they remain connected, but for some in dysfunctional situations it is important that they break away from circumstances that are binding and oppressive.

Many of us in church life have suffered through broken relationships. Historically, it has been important for various people to take a stand on issues of doctrine, heresy or morality. Some have had to separate in an effort to keep the church pure, but when all is said and done independence is not God's best. It is not good for either man or church to be alone. Paul's letter tells us that we are called to *interdependence* – that we all need one another and that God's heart beats unity. It is my belief that we need to do our part within today's confusing church scene to work for unity. This is not ecumenical niceness or finding the lowest common denominator of agreement, but believing that the unity Jesus prayed for is a real possibility. Some have looked at unity as a kind of cloning where everyone looks alike, speaks the same things and we all always agree. The picture Paul paints here is very different. Unity and diversity walk hand in hand; issues of contention are worked through; situations are addressed, and Jesus Christ is central. Unity is not perfection, but it is agreement to walk together under God's rule.

At this point, I would like to quote three sections from 1 Corinthians 12 using *The Message*. Eugene Peterson gives some helpful insights into the text.

Integration

> 'We each used to independently call our own shots, but then we entered into a large and integrated life in which he has the final say in everything.' (verse 13)

Paul paints the picture here of all the parts being joined into the whole for greater effectiveness. There are many parts, but these many parts make up one body. To miss this important truth is to be robbed of the greatness of God's plan which He aims to fulfil through His church. There is only one body and Jesus is the only head. He should always have the final say.

Identification

> *'The old labels we once used to identify ourselves – labels like Jew or Greek, slave or free – are no longer useful. We need something larger, more comprehensive.'*   (verse 13)

Increasingly, our identification should be as followers of Jesus. Our local churches should be as important to us as they are to God, but certain labels are no longer useful. This is where the rubber hits the road for many churches that belong to a specific grouping or network which has its own particular flavour. When we talk of losing our identity in Jesus it can produce a measure of insecurity in those who are comfortable with their current identity. Certainly this passage is not suggesting that all churches should come together under some new governmental umbrella, but it does encourage us to desire greater levels of co-operation and togetherness across our cities and regions. The truth is that as we are identified in our world, we need something larger and more comprehensive that says, 'We are God's people.'

Illustration

> *'The way God designed our bodies is a* **model** *for understanding our lives together as a church: every part dependent on every other part, the parts we mention and the parts we don't, the parts we see and the parts we don't. If one part hurts, every other part is involved in the hurt and in the healing. If one part flourishes, every part enters into the exuberance. You are Christ's body – that's who you are. You must never forget this.'*
> (verses 25–27).

If only we could grasp this illustration. We are all part of one body and we are all very different. Some of us are visible and some aren't, but we are all indispensable. Just as it is ludicrous to consider limbs of a body vying for independence or greater influence, it is equally ridiculous to think that we could 'go it alone'. One of the above sentences really gripped my attention: *'Every other part is involved in the **hurt** and in the **healing**.'* Too often we have been involved in the hurt. May we make ourselves available for the healing.

Chapter 17

Stewarding Our Resources

(1 Corinthians 16)

On first reading, these verses appear to be simply drawing a few final thoughts together after the meaty issues that were addressed earlier in the letter. However, on closer scrutiny something crucial to the whole epistle is revealed. In a few verses, Paul highlights three of the greatest resources that any church will have. They are, money, opportunities and people.

We have already looked into the subject of money and generosity, but this chapter reveals a very important issue with regard to all the resources that the church may possess. It is the issue of 'stewardship' – a word that needs some explanation in today's world.

When God gives resources to His church, it is vitally important that they are not wasted. In fact, it is essential that they produce as much fruit as possible. A steward is a person who is entrusted with the management of estates or affairs. He or she does this for someone else and has no personal ownership. In Corinthians 4:1–2 Paul speaks of servants or stewards who are entrusted with the secret things of God. The authorised version translates these words as 'stewards of the mysteries of God'.

In the Old Testament, Joseph was given stewardship throughout his life. He was not too wise in stewarding God's mysteries in his early, youthful days, when God gave him dreams about his future destiny. However, as time progressed and due to the sufferings he had to endure, he became a faithful steward. He oversaw and managed the household of

Potiphar and when he was wrongly accused of an immoral relationship with Potiphar's wife, he handled himself with integrity. This led to a period of wrongful imprisonment, but here again he faithfully handled that over which God had given him authority. Eventually, he walked into the destiny for which he was born: stewarding for Pharaoh the huge resources of Egypt and saving the nation and many people from disaster.

The word 'steward' literally means 'under-rower' and paints the picture of the slaves who rowed the huge Roman galleys. These slaves were definitely *not* in charge. It was simply their task to keep rowing on behalf of the captain; they had no rights of their own. The church is the household of faith and we, like Joseph, are called to be faithful managers and stewards.

Money (verses 1–4)

1 Corinthians 16 follows a strong doctrinal passage on the resurrection. We now move from doctrine to duty. Our faith always needs a practical outworking; vision always needs to be resourced. Having already given some attention to these verses, I would like to reference two simple things.

Firstly, *giving is an act of worship*. In Philippians 4:18 Paul describes a monetary gift in the following way. Gifts are, '. . . *a fragrant offering, an acceptable sacrifice, pleasing to God.*' In the channelling of our money for particular projects or the needs of people, we should never lose sight of this central principle.

Secondly, *giving is a grace*. When all is said and done our giving can only ever flow from that which God has already supplied us with. 2 Corinthians 8:1 says, '*And now, brothers, we want you to know about the grace that God has given the Macedonian churches.*' God's grace poured out upon us demands that we be good stewards of that which He has liberally given to us. By faith, when we give, we actually gain. This is the principle of Kingdom economics that makes no sense at all to the natural mind. If our hearts remain closed then our hands will remain closed. If our hearts are open towards God, then our hands are more likely to be open towards His people and to the needs of others. The stewarding of our money will ultimately show where our hearts are.

Opportunities (verses 5–9)

It is also vitally important that we learn how to steward our
time. It is so easy to waste time or even kill time. Time is a gift
from God. There are occasions when the Lord will present us
with a window of opportunity to achieve something for Him;
if we are careless about stewarding our time, then we may well
miss these divine appointments, because by implication, we
are probably more interested in 'doing our own thing'. An
'opportunity' is defined as 'a fit or convenient time; an
occasion that is favourable to us.' Paul recognised that God
had given him a great opportunity in the city of Ephesus
(verse 8). He refers to this God-given opportunity as a 'great
door' that had opened up to him. Doors are usually entrances
into new things and Paul was sure that a door to take the
gospel into Ephesus had opened for him. This meant that
others doors were less important to him at that particular
time.

We need to learn how to discern which 'doors' are priorities
for us. Even seasoned believers struggle with the whole issue
of guidance. Is the door before us God-given or a diversion?
Should I go through the door now? Shall I try pushing the
door to see if it will open? After all, not all our ideas and plans
are from God, and our decision-making can often be tainted
by hidden agendas. When Paul found his *'great door for
effective work'*, he opened himself up to misunderstanding
from the Corinthian church. Notice the words that Paul uses
in this passage: *'Perhaps I will stay with you a while, or even spend
the winter'* (verse 6). This is hardly the language of a focused
apostle. He then wrote, *'I hope to spend some time with you, if the
Lord permits'* (verse 7). He chose words that allowed him
flexibility and adjustment with his plans. This left him open
to criticism. In fact, there is evidence that Paul had to revise
his plans at least twice and because of this was accused of
having wrong motives (2 Corinthians 1:15–17). Some felt that
he had not honoured his commitments. Paul had to prioritise
his time. He was certain of the fact that God had opened up
the work in Ephesus (verse 8) and this was his priority. Paul
could not arrange his diary according to need. There was no
doubt that the many needs within the Corinthian church
could have been a full-time job for him, but Paul only had one

life to live and an allotted number of years in which to minister. He needed to make the most of every opportunity God gave him. In Ephesians 5:15 he says, *'Be very careful, then, how you live – not as unwise but as wise, making the most of every opportunity, because the days are evil.'*

With regard to guidance there are two extremes that we need to avoid. Firstly, failing to make decisions because we are afraid of making mistakes, and secondly, making impulsive decisions and rushing ahead too quickly. People tend to fall into one of these two categories. It is essential for all of us that we move forward, but we need to do so in consultation and with care. People in ministry have a tendency to move forward too quickly based on impulse, a Bible verse, or a circumstance. If God is really opening up an effective door, it will become obvious to those to whom we are accountable.

We therefore need to make the most of every opportunity and wisely steward our time. While writing these words I am sitting in the departure lounge of Gatwick Airport, having arrived early (a habit that tends to annoy my family). I am now seeking to use my time wisely. I have to confess that I would normally spend two or three hours doing very little, walking through all the shops, but buying nothing. So now I am smugly redeeming some of that time and feeling good about it, hoping that I will very soon find an effective 'open gate' with no delays! Time is a precious gift. Let us do our best to steward every opportunity and in doing so, please God.

People (verses 10–24)

The final verses of 1 Corinthians 16 give us an insight into how Paul operated. He concludes by recognising that his life is joined to many people who have helped and assisted him along the way. Relationships were important to Paul. The names of almost seventy people who worked alongside him can be found in Paul's letters.

Sometimes a God-given door will open to us, but even then it is essential that right relationships be in place. I was amazed recently to read the following verses:

'Now when I went to Troas to preach the gospel of Christ and found that the Lord had opened the door for me, I still had no

*peace of mind because I did not find my brother Titus there. So
I said goodbye to them and went on to Macedonia.'*

(2 Corinthians 2:12–13)

The implications in these verses are incredible. Could it be
that there are what seem to be perfectly good doors that we
would be unwise to go through if there is no relationship in
place? This has to do with timing. Many have gone through
doors prematurely, only to find, years later, isolation and
disillusionment.

Stewarding relationships is very important and Paul mentions a number of people who have been essential to him on
his journeys. They are very different, but equally valuable
people, each with a specific attribute that was helpful to
Paul: Timothy – faithful; Apollos – favoured; Stephanus –
foundational; Aquila and Priscilla – flexible.

Money and opportunities have little value without people.
Let's take a look at these characters in a little more detail.

▶ *Timothy (verse 10)*
Eventually Timothy was to take the place of Paul at Ephesus.
As Paul's spiritual son, he carried on the work of the Lord with
faithfulness.

▶ *Apollos (verse 12)*
Even though a section of the church was Apollos' fan club,
Paul was secure enough to want him on the team. In fact he
'strongly urged him to go with his brothers' (verse 12). Notice the
response Apollos gives to this apostolic request. Verse 12
continues, *'He was quite unwilling to go now ...'* He was clearly
his own man and though he took Paul's request seriously, he
was not going to move just because Paul said so. This was not a
rebellious refusal, in fact he promised he would go when he
had the opportunity. This should shed light for us on what it
looks like when ministry relationships operate maturely.

▶ *Stephanus (verse 15)*
This man and his family were foundational people who had
worked hard in the life of the church. They devoted themselves to the service of the saints and often toiled to the point
of exhaustion. They were the kind of people that refreshed

the church rather than drained it. Paul writes, *'Such men deserve recognition'* (verse 18). Sometimes we fail to thank those who are always with us. We often spend time with people who consistently need help, but forget to thank or honour the solid, dependable people who give us tireless support.

▶ *Aquila and Priscilla (verse 15)*

This was a husband and wife team. They first met Paul in Corinth after leaving Rome. They are mentioned six times in the New Testament and interestingly Priscilla's name is first in four of them. She was perhaps the more gifted of the two. They moved their house and their business to support Paul in Ephesus. They opened their home for the church to meet together. Later they assisted Timothy in Ephesus. They were flexible in their attitude and dedicated to the kingdom. Willingly, they served whoever was leading at a given time. The stewarding of relationships needs to be a priority in the church today.

Chapter 18

The Clay Element

Whenever I think of clay I think of my old eccentric art teacher. I have to say that the Christian message had not at this point in my life, produced a full transforming work. I enjoyed, along with others, bringing disruption to the class. A friend and I noticed that when our teacher became angry he would stamp around the room. For the whole period we produced a graph of the number of stamps he would make, showing a correlation between anger and stamping. We felt our exercise might help someone with anger management in the years ahead.

The second memory I have is of the days when we were given clay in class. We were, of course, supposed to produce a bowl or vase, but when the teacher turned his back the cry would go up, 'Sir, we've lost our clay.' Perturbed by this outburst he would eventually look heavenward for inspiration, only to see the ceiling splattered with the 'lost' clay. The clay would stick for a while, but would usually fall before break time. On the few occasions when we took the lesson more seriously, I remember trying to use a potter's wheel. It always looked so easy when the experts were at work, but as I placed my clay on the wheel it flopped over and twisted into a highly unusual but creative shape. Needless to say, I didn't continue with art but I did learn something about clay!

Today, clay has a special meaning for me. The last time my dad preached in our church in Lincoln, he brought a picture with him. It was an oil painting of numerous pots of differing shapes and sizes, produced by one of the artists in our church. The richly coloured painting became a visual aid for that morning. My dad remained seated while he spoke because he was ill and disease had taken its toll. His voice was weak and his breathing difficult. He took us that morning to 2 Corinthians 4 – the passage about clay jars. However, as my dad began to speak I recognised that this passage was not focusing on the jars at all. Another focus began to emerge. At the time I didn't see it as clearly as I do today. I was concerned about the 'clay jar' about the 'tent' – our bodies.

Here was my dad in his very frail 'tent', and the sight was hurting me. Now, a number of years on, I can see that actually the painting wasn't the visual aid, my dad was. I caught a glimpse of something in him that day, something difficult to describe – a combination of experience, inner strength and spirituality. Yet, it was more than that. It was something bright and expensive; something that had stood the test of time. For me anyway, I had caught a glimpse of what the Bible calls 'treasure'.

> *'But we have this treasure in jars of clay, to show that this all-surpassing power is from God and not from us.'*
>
> (2 Corinthians 4:7)

The treasure

Treasure is a collection of wealth, especially of gold or jewels. It is something to be valued and prized. It is the light of God shining into our hearts carrying the glory of God through relationship with Christ. This is something that the world cannot possess: it is eternal, immovable and of great price. In fact, the Scriptures tell us that our bodies are temples of the Holy Spirit (1 Corinthians 3:16). The mystery is how such treasure can reside in jars of clay. Perhaps the answer is to do with where the glory goes. In our world so much glory goes to people. To the rich and famous, the intelligent and gifted, the articulate and funny; to sports personalities, to rock stars, designers and models; to prime ministers, presidents, kings and queens. But it is treasure in jars of clay which *'... shows that this all-surpassing power is from God and not from us'* (2 Corinthians 4:7). So does this mean that we remain 'pot-shaped' with 'pot intelligence' and 'pot gift'? No, it simply means that we make sure where the glory goes: all the glory must go to Him.

Treasure in the making

The concept of 'process' is not easy for Christians to grasp and particularly charismatics. We so often look for instant blessing, but God is a God of process. He works in us, walks with us, and works on us. In the process, pain is unavoidable. Pearls are produced when the oyster is irritated with sand. Gold is found through a combination of pressure and mining. Riches are often stored in dark and secret places (Isaiah 45:3). Paul, in his first letter, is preparing the Corinthians to do some quality building in the church. *'If any man builds on this foundation using gold, silver, costly stones, wood, hay or straw his work will be shown for what it is, because the Day will bring it to light. It will be revealed with fire, and the fire will test the quality of each man's work'* (1 Corinthians 3:12–13). It seems to me that all believers have treasure within and are called to build with quality, a life that reflects this inner life. We have been prepared for good works and all the glory goes to Him.

Painful paradox

The Christian life is never easy. It is a roller-coaster of events and circumstances, good and bad, and is not usually fair. Certainly the clay element is in all of us, but notice the perspective of Paul:

Hard pressed on every side (verse 8)	but not crushed (verse 8)
Perplexed (verse 8)	but not in despair (verse 8)
Persecuted (verse 9)	but not abandoned (verse 9)
Struck down (verse 9)	but not destroyed (verse 9)

We are all wired differently. I have a tendency to emphasise the hard-pressed column, but the truth is that there is always a 'but'. The process can be painful, but God's promises are perfect and never fail.

> *'Because we know that the one who raised the Lord Jesus Christ from the dead will also raise us with Jesus and present us with you in his presence.'*　　　(2 Corinthians 4:14)

Breaking the jars

There is a story in Judges about a man called Gideon. He was clearly clay-like, with a huge inferiority complex. Even though God Himself promised He would be with him, Gideon required signs to prove that this was really true. Pot-shaped people require many fleeces. In order that Gideon did not think that victory was due to his leadership skills or to the size of his army, God told him to cut back his troops. Imagine the Lord telling a general, *'You have too many men'* (Judges 7:4). I am convinced Gideon wanted his army to be as large and powerful as possible. But God was interested in where the glory would go. The battle was not going to be won by the strong or the brave. It was going to be won by men who knew how to lap water in a way that showed their readiness to be obedient and put their faith in God. The huge army was cut down to three hundred. The battle tactics were interesting. The army was split into three groups and issued with trumpets, jars and torches. With much noise and passionate faith in God, the enemy was routed.

But it is the image of the broken jars that gets my attention. As the jars were broken, the light of hundreds of torches penetrated the darkness. As lives are broken in consecration to God, the treasure is revealed, and God gets the glory and the devil gets a beating.

A New Testament story also comes to mind of a woman offering her worship to God. She took a box of expensive ointment, her treasured possession, and released a fragrant anointing oil that covered the head of her Lord. In this act of sacrifice, love and devotion were poured out.

Clay jars do begin to wear out, the glazing fades and the outer beauty diminishes. But the truth is that the reverse is happening on the inside. It seems that the more the outside fades, the inside shines even more brightly. The troubles of life eventually find a perspective as the eternal glory begins to appear. We look at the outside and get discouraged. but God always looks on the heart. What we see now is passing, fading and temporary, but the part which we only catch a glimpse of, is eternal. Don't be overly concerned when the glazing fades; the treasure inside will look all the more beautiful.

'Therefore, we do not lose heart.'   (2 Corinthians 4:16)

You have chosen the foolish to confound the wise
The humble and lowly, despised in their eyes,
You have taken the weak, so that even angels seek
The secret of the vessel made of clay.

And all the glory goes to You
And all the honour belongs to You
You have taken the weak
So that even angels seek
The secret of the vessel made of clay
The secret of the vessel made of clay.

The Twenty-first Century?

Many people see the problems of the church, but few offer a solution. There are always the 'prophets of doom' who wonder whether the church in the West can survive for many more years. I believe there is a lot of healthy debate at present concerning the nature of the church and how it should be expressed. In this book I have sought to acknowledge the weaknesses, but my overriding conviction is that Jesus is building His church and that the gates of hell will not overcome it (Matthew 16:19). I find it inconceivable that that which Jesus instigated will disappear into obscurity. In fact, I am looking for a highly effective church breaking through into new territory in this next century. So often we make our assessments through the filters of our own experiences. Often when people are hurting or disillusioned, the way that they perceive things is easily tainted. It is amazing to me that the prophet Elijah, who had called fire down on the prophets of Baal and seen incredible miracles, should some time later be sitting under a broom tree wishing that he could die. He had lost his perspective and lost the plot because of the taunts of Jezebel, who had made him feel impotent and ineffective.

Today is the day to listen to the stories of what God is doing in and through His church worldwide and receive fresh encouragement. It is a day to step back a little in order to see the salvation of our God. God has been restoring His people and this is not a time to retreat under our broom tree. We need to take back that which the enemy has taken from us. Terry Virgo puts into words the heart cry of many of us in his book, *Does the Future Have a Church?*:

> 'My appeal, therefore, is that rather than give up on the church and anticipate her inevitable demise, we give our best energies to her success, knowing that Christ is determined to have a glorious bride, worthy of his own majesty and might.'[25]

If Paul had allowed the revelation of the church that had graciously been given him to be affected by disappointments and trials, or by the prevailing culture of his day, we would not, at the beginning of this century, still be standing.

In conclusion, may I simply make mention of some things that are well worth revisiting. Many of these have proven helpful to me during thirty years of ministry, but it is my belief that fresh revelation can come again to these important truths. The unfolding of this revelation based on firm foundations of the past, may well contribute to the success of the church in the years that are to come. Each of the following are suggestions for further discussion and prayer.

Things to thoughtfully revisit

- Gifts of the Holy Spirit and their release today
- Communion and meaningful fellowship
- Body ministry and the development of people
- Discipleship and mentoring
- Love for one another
- Unity for territory's sake
- Order and discipline in the church
- The training of new leaders
- Stewardship of what God gives us
- Purity and holiness as a lifestyle
- Suffering and identification with the world
- Christian influence in the market place
- The Ephesians 4 ministries
- What it means to preach the cross of Christ
- The importance of the resurrection

'And that's about it, friends. Be cheerful. Keep things in good repair. Keep your spirits up. Think in harmony. Be agreeable. Do all that, and the God of love and peace will be with you for sure. Greet one another with a holy embrace. All the brothers and sisters here say hello. The amazing grace of the Master, Jesus Christ, the extravagant love of God, the intimate friendship of the Holy Spirit, be with all of you.'

(2 Corinthians 16:11–14, *The Message*)

Notes

1. *Fourth Wave*, Hodder & Stoughton, London 1993, p. 20.
2. *The Message Bible*, NAV Press, 2002, p. 2064.
3. *Ibid.*
4. *NIV Bible Commentary*, Hodder & Stoughton, Zondervan Publishing House, 1994, p. 607.
5. G. Campbell Morgan, *The Messages of the Books of the Bible*, Hodder & Stoughton, p. 131.
6. *New Century Bible*, Nelson Word Bibles, Word Publishing, 1991 p. 1321.
7. John R.W. Stott, *God's New Society*, IVP, 1979, quoted in *Does the Future Have a Church?*, Terry Virgo, Kingsway Publications, 2003, p. 104.
8. *The Cross*, Sovereign World, 2002, p. 55.
9. *New Dictionary of Theology*, InterVarsity Press, 1988, p. 583.
10. *Systematic Theology*, Wayne Grudem, InterVarsity Press, Zondervan Publishing House 1994, p. 608.
11. Frank Morrison, *Who Moved the Stone?*, Faber & Faber, reprint Grand Rapids: Zondervan, 1958.
12. *A New Testament Study, Be Wise*, Colorado: Chariot Victor Publishing, 2003, p. 76.
13. Warren Wiersbe, *Be Wise*, Chariot Victor Publishing, 2003, p. 82.
14. *Top 10 of Everything*, Monarch Books, Mill Hill, London and Grand Rapids, Michigan, 2003, p. 39.
15. *Ibid.*
16. *Hands of Jesus*, Denmark: Powerhouse Publishing, 2003, p. 69.
17. *Prophetic Evangelism*, Milton Keynes: Authentic Media, 2004.

18. *A New Testament Study, Be Wise*, Colorado Springs: Chariot Victor Publishing, 2003, p. 111.
19. Eugene H. Peterson, *The Message Bible*, NAV Press, 2002, p. 2081.
20. *Beyond Suffering, Where Is God When it Hurts*, Marshall Pickering, 1998, p. 76.
21. Herbert Carson, *Facing Suffering*, Evangelical Press, 1978, p. 63.
22. *The Dictionary of Theology*, Leicester: InterVarsity Press, 1988, p. 399.
23. F.B. Meyer, *Our Daily Homily*, Morgan & Scott Limited.
24. Matthew Henry, *Commentary on the Whole Bible*, Marshall Morgan & Scott, 1960, p. 617.
25. *Does the Future Have a Church?*, Kingsway Publications, 2003.

If you have enjoyed this book and would like to help us to send a copy of it and many other titles to needy pastors in the **Third World**, please write for further information or send your gift to:

Sovereign World Trust
PO Box 777, Tonbridge
Kent TN11 0ZS
United Kingdom

or to the **'Sovereign World'** distributor in your country.

Visit our website at **www.sovereign-world.org**
for a full range of Sovereign World books.